To Be Human
Before God

To Be Human Before God

Insights from Biblical Spirituality

Michael D. Guinan, O.F.M.

A Liturgical Press Book

THE LITURGICAL PRESS
Collegeville, Minnesota

Cover design by Ann Blattner

Cover illustration by Ethel Boyle

1	2	3	4	5	6	7	8

Library of Congress Cataloging-in-Publication Data

Guinan, Michael D.
    To be human before God : insights from biblical spirituality / Michael D. Guinan.
       p.   cm.
    ISBN 0-8146-2207-0
    1. Man (Christian theology)   2. Bible—Criticism, interpretation, etc.   3. Spirituality—Catholic Church.   I. Title.
BT701.2.G85   1994
233—dc20
                                    94-1900
                                      CIP

Contents

Preface

What does it mean to be human? This question is a central one in any spirituality, affecting variously how we relate to God, to others, to the world, and to ourselves. The question has two aspects which, while they can be distinguished, are closely interconnected: (1) how do we understand, image, and conceptualize what it means to be a human being before God?; (2) how are we to live this out in and through our different relationships?

As we seek answers from the Christian tradition, we turn of necessity to the Scriptures. There we find an immediate answer: to be human is to be a weak, fallen creature prone to sin and death. In this condition we cry out to God and God enters our world to save us. As true as this answer is, recent Scripture study has made it increasingly clear that in itself it is an inadequate answer. To be human is also to be created by God, to be God's image entrusted with responsibility to share in God's dominion over creation. We have not only been saved by God, we have also been blessed by God.

The recovery of this *blessing* tradition—with its distinct but interrelated strands of creation, royal, and wisdom thought—poses challenges for spirituality. How is it to be related to the much more familiar *saving* tradition? This challenge is evident when, for example, we consider two writers who have attended seriously to the spiritual dimensions of the blessing tradition: Matthew Fox and Walter Brueggemann. Fox, who focuses more on the creation aspect of blessing and embraces it with enthusiasm, does so to the neglect of the saving tradition. Brueggemann, who is more taken with the royal dimensions of the blessing tradition, regards it with no little suspicion and hesitation in favor of the saving tradition. While each scholar has made important contributions, I do not find that either of them adequately appreciates the diversity of the biblical material.

How do we proceed then, trying, on the one hand, to hear and respect the biblical text as it presents these two very different traditions, and seeking, on the other hand, to consider their implications for spirituality? Since I know of no work that consistently tries to do this, it will be the governing project of this book. As we proceed in our search, we will find that a large number of issues will surface and our perceptions of them will be transformed. Since I am firmly convinced of the close connection between theology and spirituality, I will usually devote attention to the former before asking about its applications and challenges to the latter. Sometimes these will be more obvious; at other times, more discussion may be necessary.

I began to develop this material in the context of a course I have team-taught over the years with Francis Baur, O.F.M., a course called "Christian Spirituality in Contemporary Biblical and Theological Perspective." The dialog between us as we've taught together has been very enriching. One might, then, with curiosity and benefit, also read Baur's book, *Life in Abundance: A Contemporary Spirituality* (Ramsey, N.J.: Paulist, 1983) in conjuction with this one. My work has also developed out of numerous dialogs with many others whom I have met during courses, retreats (with priests, sisters, and lay people), recollections, and parish workshops—both in the United States and in the Philippines (during the six summers I have been graced to work there). These many persons have left their imprint upon me and given me encouragement; I owe them all my thanks.

The biblical text I will use throughout is that of the New American Bible. At times I modify it slightly where a more literal reading is necessary for the point at hand.

Michael D. Guinan, O.F.M.
Franciscan School of Theology
Berkeley, California

Abbreviations

BIB	*Biblical Theology Bulletin*
Int	*Interpretation*
JBL	*Journal of Biblical Literature*
JETS	*Journal of the Evangelical Theological Society*
JSOT	*Journal for the Study of the Old Testament*
NJBC	*New Jerome Biblical Commentary,* R. E. Brown, et al., eds. (Englewood Cliffs, N.J.: Prentice-Hall, 1990).
RStRev	*Religious Studies Review*
SR	*Studies in Religion*
TBT	*The Bible Today*
THAT	*Theologisches Handwörterbuch zum Alten Testament,* E. Jenni & C. Westermann, eds. (Munich: C. Kaiser, 1971 [vol. 1], 1976 [vol. 2]).
WW	*Word and World*

Chapter 1

Spirituality and Spiritualities

Spirituality is definitely "in." Within the religious sphere, we may note the proliferation of religious books and articles dealing with spiritual topics; the catalogs of taped lectures and retreat conferences available; the popularity and spread of different kinds of retreat experiences. Beyond the narrowly religious, a similar impulse manifests itself in our culture at large in the range of personal growth and human potential concerns, as well as the various "New Age" movements.[1] People are interested in living fuller, deeper, more personal human lives. Even this casual glance across our culture—in both its religious and secular manifestations—points to a great hunger and thirst for more authentic "spiritual life."

Levels of Spirituality

But what do we mean by spirituality? Because of the wide range of movements and approaches, the term can be vague and elusive, used in a variety of ways.[2] All too often we jump into discussions presuming everyone means the same thing when using the same term. Methodologically, it is always wise to begin by defining terms. Without attempting to deal with all the possible meanings, we can understand spirituality in at least four different ways, corresponding to four levels on

1. M. F. Bednarowski, "Literature of the New Age: A Review of Representative Sources," *RStRev* 17 (1991) 209–16.
2. C. Jones, G. Wainwright, E. Yarnold, *The Study of Spirituality* (New York/Oxford: Oxford University Press, 1986) xxii.

1

which the question can be approached. These move from the most general to the most concrete:

(1) On the first and most general level, spirituality deals in some way with the human response to transcendent reality. This type of response is "the unique and personal response of individuals to all that calls them to integrity and transcendence."[3] While different writers may emphasize different aspects of spirituality,[4] general agreement exists that it "has something to do with the unification of life by reference to something beyond the individual person."[5]

Whether one studies Christianity, Buddhism, Islam, or Native American spiritualities, the experience of transcendent reality is a common element. The findings of most comparative religious studies and psychologies of religion bear this out.

(2) On the second level, both the human response and the transcendent reality being responded to are taken seriously. The two poles of the relationship are held together and studied together. Here it is necessary to discuss not only the human response but also the way in which a particular community context and/or tradition understands transcendent reality, often (but not necessarily) defined as God. On this level, we can distinguish and speak meaningfully, for example, of Christian spirituality, Buddhist spirituality, Hindu, Islamic, or whatever.[6]

From this point on, our concern will be only with Christian spirituality which we can define concisely as: our life in the Spirit of God.[7] In the Scriptures, the basic meaning of

3. S. Schneiders, "Theology and Spirituality: Strangers, Rivals, or Partners?" *Horizons* 13 (1986) 264.
4. In addition to Schneiders' article just cited, see also J. Alexander, "What Do Recent Writers Mean by Spirituality?" *Spirituality Today* 32 (1980) 247–56; R. Hardy, "Christian Spirituality Today: Notes on Its Meaning," *Spiritual Life* 28 (1982) 151–59; W. Principe, "Toward defining spirituality," *SR* 12 (1983) 123–41.
5. S. Schneiders, "Theology and Spirituality," 266.
6. For a brief discussion (with bibliography) of Jewish, Islamic, Hindu, Buddhist, African, and Amerindian spiritualities, see section IX of C. Jones, et al., *The Study of Spirituality*, 491–518.
7. The use of the term *spirituality* in a technical sense, referring to

"spirit" is very concrete. Whether referring to the Hebrew *ruaḥ*, the Greek *pneuma*, or the Latin *spiritus*, the basic reference is to "wind" or "breath." In his death and resurrection, Jesus "breathed out" his spirit—his breath—on all: "And bowing his head, he handed over the spirit" (John 19:30). When he appeared to his frightened disciples in the upper room on the evening of the day of the resurrection, "[Jesus] breathed on them and said to them, 'Receive the Holy Spirit' " (John 20:22). Jesus' followers now share the same life-breath, the same principle of life. We are filled with his spirit. The same breath that animated (and still animates) Jesus, now animates us. We live in, through, and with the power of the same breath-spirit as Jesus. "Whoever is joined to the Lord becomes one spirit with him" (1 Cor 6:17). Earlier in the same letter, Paul makes an instructive and significant distinction between the "spiritual person," and the "natural person" who does not accept "what pertains to the Spirit of God" (1 Cor 2:14-15). The Holy Spirit, the Holy Breath of Jesus is within us, motivating, empowering, animating our lives (Rom 5:5).

"Spiritual," then, refers to the whole of our existence as Christian, as filled with the Spirit of Christ. We are filled so much with this Spirit that Paul can say, "I live, no longer I, but Christ lives in me" (Gal 2:20). As Christians, we follow Christ, we share his death and resurrection (Phil 2:10), we

---

the way in which one lives out the Christian life, is of fairly recent origin, dating only from seventeenth century France. At that time it was distinguished from dogmatic theology (dealing with the systematic and philosophical elaboration of Christian doctrine) and moral theology (dealing with principles of ethical behavior, conscience, law, sin, etc.). While it did not have to be so, in fact moral theology tended to concentrate more on the negative aspects of Christian existence (sin, types of sin, conditions for sin, etc.) leaving *spirituality* to focus more on the positive aspects of growth in the Christian life (asceticism, virtue, mystical life). In this context, the interior aspects (prayer, meditation, detachment from the material) were of primary concern. While this kind of approach had some limited usefulness, it does not do justice to a more biblically based understanding of the Christian life. On the history of the usage of the term *spirituality,* see S. Schneiders, "Theology and Spirituality," 257–60; C. Jones, et al., *The Study of Spirituality,* xxiv–xxvi; W. Principe, "Toward defining spirituality," 130–35.

breathe with his breath. Christian spirituality deals with the progressive transformation of our whole lives by the power and presence of Christ's Spirit.

Obviously then, spirituality does not refer only to our interior lives nor primarily to mental and rational activity. Within Christian history, various movements have arisen which have stressed the role of understanding and knowledge. This gnostic (from *gnosis,* the Greek word for knowlege[8]) impulse is and continues to be a temptation in the Christian life: "I *know* more so I am saved, so I am better than others." But spirituality is not exclusively or merely interior, rational activity. While it surely includes these, it involves my whole person and our whole life.

Closely connected with this is another problem. "Spiritual" should not be confused with the distinction between matter and spirit, body and soul. When this is done, the "spiritual" life is primarily (if not exclusively) the life of the soul. The body and materiality in general is spurned, distrusted, and despised.[9] While this dichotomizing has happened all too often in the history of Christian spirituality, it is quite foreign to the biblical perspective. There, as we have seen, "spiritual" refers to the whole person—body and soul—living under the influence of God's Spirit. In the biblical view, matter or material reality is not opposed to this Spirit; only sin is. When Paul speaks of our whole person under the dominion of sin, weakness, and death, at times he calls this "living according to the flesh" (e.g., Rom 8:5-10; Gal 5:16-26). This use of "flesh" should not be identified with "the body." Introducing the body-soul distinction here is anachronistic and inappropriate, and violates the Scriptures.[10]

Christian spirituality, then, deals with the whole person—body and soul, thoughts and feelings, emotions and passions,

8. For a brief introduction to Gnosticism, see P. Perkins, "Gnosticism," *NJBC,* 80:64-82.

9. Such attitudes to materiality are an additional characteristic of gnostic type spiritualities.

10. On Paul's use of the term *flesh,* see J. Fitzmyer, "Pauline Theology," *NJBC,* 82:103; see also S. Schneiders, "Theology and Spirituality," 257–58; W. Principe, "Toward defining spirituality," 130.

hopes, fears and dreams—as we live in and with the power of the Spirit. And it deals with the whole life of the whole person, calling us to live this life to the fullest. In fact, from a biblical perspective, the expression "spiritual life" is a tautology. If we are indeed truly alive, if we are truly breathing, it is with the Spirit-breath of God. If we have turned our backs on God by sin, then even if we still walk the earth, we are dying; we are under the power of death. This call and challenge of the spiritual life is not restricted to only some Christians (e.g., priests, religious) but is addressed to all. All share the same Spirit and are called to one and the same holiness. This basic fact was much stressed by Vatican Council II. Its decree on the church, *Lumen Gentium*, devotes a whole chapter (ch. 5) to developing the theme of the one call to holiness in the Spirit addressed to all.

(3) No one, however, lives "Christian spirituality" in the abstract. We all live at specific and particular moments in space and time; in other words, we live in definite historical and cultural contexts. We are part of distinct social groupings and particular religious communities into which we were born, in which we grow, relate, are educated, and come to know and experience God. Our particular contexts give us our identities and our language; they pose questions to us and challenge us; they propose models of life in seeking to respond to these questions and challenges. The concrete and changing circumstances of our lives cannot but affect the way we live out our Christian spirituality. It is on this secondary level that we can speak of different Christian spiritualities, that is, different styles, modalities, or modifications of the one common Christian call to holiness.

The various styles or modifications of the Christian life can be based on different kinds of factors. We can begin with that of time: at what point in history does one live? Here we can distinguish, for example, the spirituality of the early Church, of the Middle Ages, of the Reformation, of the nineteenth century, of the contemporary situation. Or we may consider the factor of space: where in the world do we live? We can speak of, e.g., Greek spirituality, French, Irish, Asian, or American spirituality. Some would even add a distinct "Californian" spirituality (with northern and southern being quite distinct)! Different religious traditions within Christianity offer another factor (Orthodox, Anglican, Baptist, Lutheran, Roman Catholic, etc.) as can our state in life (lay, religious, priest). Each of these contexts presents life in slightly different ways, asks slightly different questions, deals with slightly different problems, and proposes different models for inspiration and imitation.[11]

Further, in the history of the Church, certain charismatic leaders have emerged who spearheaded religious renewals during their lives, and who, through the power of their lives and examples, attracted followers down through the centuries: e.g., St. Benedict and St. Scholastica, St. Francis of Assisi and St. Clare, St. Dominic, St. Angelia Merici, St. Ignatius of Loyola. Certainly none of these individuals set out to found new "schools" of spirituality. They wanted simply to live the gospel life, to follow Christ fully and seriously to the best of their ability and in response to the needs of their times. Their example inspired others down through the ages to follow Christ as they did, and thus we speak of Benedictine, Franciscan, Dominican, Ursuline, Ignatian styles (or "schools") of spirituality.

Finally, today one hears often of other spiritualities within the Christian community. Books are written and talks are given on adolescent spirituality, Black spirituality, Hispanic spirituality, Asian spirituality, gay and lesbian spirituality, feminine spirituality. And this practice has a certain validity. Wherever a meaningful community of life exists—a sense of identity, a sharing of joy and pain, of questioning and challenge, of searching and growing—we can legitimately discern a style of Christian spirituality.

Each of us lives his or her life at the intersection of a number of these different streams. For example, I am (in no particular order): Roman Catholic, Franciscan, male, 1990s, American (further back, Irish and Italian), and Californian. While there is a validity to each of these distinctions, we should note that they exist on a secondary level. We are dealing with styles, modalities, modifications of the one basic Christian call

11. An initial discussion of these (and other) types of spirituality can be found in C. Jones, et al., *The Study of Spirituality*.

to holiness. They all exist within and manifest the richness of the Christian community through the ages.

(4) One more step brings us to the most concrete level of spirituality. On this level, each one of us is an individual and unique person and represents a unique embodiment of Christian spirituality. There has never been before, nor will there ever be again, a spirituality exactly like mine, exactly like yours. No one else has the constellation of heredity, experiences, talents, values, hopes and dreams which characterize me/you as individuals. On this level, there are as many different spiritualities as there are persons. In this sense we can say—and it is not prideful to do so—that each of us gives to God something which God did not have before and would not have if we did not give it: the unique embodiment of the risen Christ in this world here and now, that I uniquely can be. This is something, as we will discuss more below, which we have to learn to recognize, respect and develop.

Problems and Questions

The threefold level of Christian spirituality we have described (the one common Christian spirituality, the concrete modifications of it in space and time, and the unique spirituality of the individual) can be seen to correspond to the threefold distinction of nature, culture, and person. We speak, for example, of human nature, what all human beings have in common, what identifies them as distinctly human. But human nature does not exist as such; it exists only in concrete, unique human persons. Human persons, however, exist only in social groupings with language, values, experiences, etc. On the level of nature, Christian spirituality is one and the same for all; on the level of person, it is different and unique for each; on the level of culture, it is somewhat the same and somewhat different.[12] As we might expect, it is on the last level, that of culture, in which we can notice the potential for problems.

12. For a basic discussion of nature, culture, and person, see B. Malina, *The New Testament World: Insights from Cultural Anthropology* (Atlanta: John Knox Press, 1981) 7–11.

The first problem involves the relationship of a particular manifestation of Christian spiritualaity to the level above it, i.e., the basic Christian call to holiness (the relation of culture to nature). Any particular style can begin to push up and to absolutize itself. "Our" spirituality all too quickly can begin to look and sound like "the" spirituality. The danger here can be called *spiritual ethnocentrism.* We cannot lose sight of the fact that whatever style we may personally practice, it is only a secondary (but inevitable) modification of the one call to Christian life. We need to maintain some space between these two also in order to allow the vision of the Christian life to critique any and all concrete expressions of it.

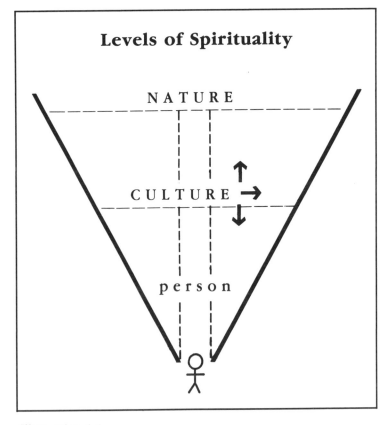

Levels of Spirituality

NATURE

CULTURE

person

Illustration 1.1

A second problem involves the relationship of differing spiritual styles to each other. Here the danger is one of *spiritual chauvinism.* "Yes, there are diverse forms of spirituality, but ours is really better than yours!" The Christian is not called to spiritual isolationism or one-upmanship. Whatever the particular style or modality, all are gifts of the one Spirit and need to be appreciated as such. The word "catholic" means "embracing the whole, the totality," and any truly catholic view of Christian spirituality will recognize that no one form or manifestation has it all; diversity manifests the richness of Christian life.

A third problem has to do with the relation of the level of culture to that just below it, that of the unique personhood of the individual. Any culture, or subculture for that matter, presents its members with certain patterns of behavior, what is or is not recommended, what is or is not accepted or tolerated. The individual is expected to conform. Dealing with the breakdown of and resistance to these culturally imposed patterns, the cultural historian Theodore Roszak has noted,

> Here, then, if we view the matter in its most general manifestation, is where the drama of contemporary disaffiliation begins: with just this painfully intense experience of *being a person* in a world that despises our personhood, a world whose policy is to grind personhood down to rubble and then to remold the pieces into obedient, efficient, and of course cheerful personnel. It is the experience of being shown what we are told is our image in a mirror society holds up to us, and then discovering that this is no mirror at all, but a crude composite photograph bearing our name . . . or perhaps our number.[13]

While Roszak is speaking here in the context of American culture, what he points to is true also of any particular Christian spiritual culture. "A good Catholic (or Anglican, or Baptist, or whatever) does not act like that, talk like that, think or feel like that." "A good priest, or minister, or religious does not do that!" The standards proposed may, of course, embody the

13. T. Roszak, *Person/Planet: The Creative Disintegration of Industrial Society* (Garden City, N.Y.: Doubleday/Anchor Press, 1979) xxvii–xxviii.

wisdom of the ages, but they may also "grind our personhood
down to rubble and then remold the pieces into obedient, ef-
ficient and, of course cheerful personnel" who should smile
and say, "Thank you, Jesus." Like everything else, these patterns and standards must be questioned and tested in the Spirit;
cultures tend to swallow up persons.

Finally, a fourth problem needs to be noted in regard to
the unique spirituality each one of us is called to realize. Not
only are there pressures "outside"—from our general culture
and from our particular religious culture—eager to take it away,
but perhaps the biggest problem comes from "inside." We can
be much too eager to give it away. Living a full Christian life
takes courage. No one has ever lived my Christian life before.
There will be doubt, confusion, uncertainty, and struggle. We
have to be open to the God who calls us out of comfortable
"nows" into unknown futures (Gen 12:1-3).[14] Jesus calls his
disciples, "Come, follow me" (e.g., Mark 1:16-20; Matt 4:18-
20; John 1:35-46). This is a frightening call involving risk and
challenging our responsibility. So we are tempted to give up
our responsibility to anyone—person or institution—who will
take it. "When I tell you what to do, you can be sure that it
is right, that it is God's will!" We ask, "What does the priest
say? the Pope? the religious superior? the Bible?" On the basis
of legitimate religious authority, we can create religious mon-
sters who swallow up our freedom in exhange for a security
blanket that wraps us warmly and lets us sleep so that we do
not have to worry about hearing the voice of God calling us
to new and ever fuller life.

The bottom line is this: how much life are we willing to
risk? how much (or how little) are we willing to settle for? How
seriously do we take the call of Christ who came that we might
have life, life in abundance (John 10:10)?[15] This is the basic
question of Christian spirituality.

14. See M. Guinan, *The Pentateuch,* Message of Biblical Spirituality
1 (Collegeville, Minn.: The Liturgical Press, 1990) 85–88, for a discussion of some temptations against the journey of faith as seen in the accounts of Israel's wandering in the wilderness.
15. This is the recurring theme of F. Baur, *Life in Abundance: A Contemporary Spirituality* (New York/Ramsey, N.J.: Paulist Press, 1983).

Chapter 2

Human Before God

Christian spirituality has to do with life, the fullness of life breathed out upon us by Christ in and through the Spirit. Each one of us is called as a unique individual to embody Christ's presence in the world, in our world. But does this not begin to sound a bit self-centered? Are we not in danger of falling into a spiritual "rugged individualism?"[1] That depends on how one understands being an individual person in the world. The meaning of human life and human existence is a very important and very basic issue in any spirituality. Our task here is to survey the teaching of Scripture on this subject.

An Individual in Relationship

When we ask about the human person, our first impulse may be to say that a human is a creature composed of body and soul, the body referring to the material part and the soul to the spiritual part. As indicated in the last chapter, this dualistic distinction, with its basis in the Greek philosophical tradition, is not always helpful in approaching biblical categories.[2]

1. The dangers and problems of this in American culture have been well discussed in R. Bellah, et al., *Habits of the Heart: Individualism and Commitment in American Life* (Berkeley, Calif.: University of California, 1985). See also the reviews of this by J. Wilson, B. Hargrove, and J. Hartt in *RStRev* 14 (1988) 304–10.
2. For the potentially harmful effects of this kind of dualism on Christian spirituality, see F. Baur, *Life in Abundance: A Contemporary Spirituality* (New York/Ramsey, N.J.: Paulist, 1983) 39–66.

The Self

How does the Bible understand human existence in the world? We will begin with the human being as an individual. The ancient biblical view recognized that a living human being is a rich and complex phenomenon which cannot be explained by handy formulas. Instead, we must circle around, seeing the person first from one angle, then from another, and from another after that. In this way an overall impression is formed which is richer and more multifaceted than any simple, one-angle view. It is further true that whatever perspective one may take at a given time, it can be used to refer to the whole, living person. This way of approaching things has been termed "stereometric thinking."[3]

From one perspective, the person can be viewed as "body" or "flesh" (Hebrew, *basar*). This is not "body" in the sense of the material principle; it refers rather to the whole, living, human person viewed—as it were—from the outside. The "body" also highlights what we have in common with other creatures, humans and animals. Since the "flesh" is the soft part of the body (the bones are the solid part), at times it indicates human existence in its weakness (e.g., Job 34:14-15; Gen 6:3; Ps 78:39).

From another angle, the person is seen as "soul" (*nephesh*). Again, it would be wrong and misleading to confuse this with the immaterial principle of Greek philosophy. "Soul" also refers to the whole, living, human person, but viewed—as it were—from the inside. The basic meaning of *nephesh* is "throat" (e.g., Isa 5:14; Hab 2:5), where experiences of hunger and thirst are felt (Ps 107:5, 9). From this, *nephesh* comes to be the organ of longing and desire welling up from deep within. "As the hind longs for the running waters, so my *nephesh* longs for you, O God" (Ps 42:2). While "throat" is not always the best translation for *nephesh* (neck, life, person, self are other possiblities), it might be good to keep it in the back of our minds. This concrete, embodied meaning can be a healthy corrective to our tendency to overspiritualize when we come across the translation "soul" in the Bible.

3. See the discussion in H. W. Wolff, *Anthropology of the Old Testament* (Philadelphia: Fortress, 1974) 7–8.

Also, one can be seen as "breath" (*ruaḥ*) which flows out
from within us. We spoke of this in the last chapter. God gives
breath to those that dwell on earth (Isa 42:5); living creatures
depend on God's breath (Gen 2:7; Ps 104:28). When the wind
blows over the dry bones, they come to life (Ezek 37:6-10).
Ruaḥ is the vital force of life.

Perhaps the most important anthropological element is that
of "heart" (*leb, lebab*). For us the heart is the seat of our emotional life, of our feelings. In the Bible, the idea is much richer.
While the proper locus of feelings are the intestines (e.g., the
"bowels of mercy"), feelings may also flow from the heart
(e.g., Prov 15:13; 17:22) as do wishes and desires (e.g., Ps 21:2;
Prov 6:25—in this, *leb* is similar to *nephesh* and *ruaḥ*). But the
heart also thinks and understands. Thus "the intelligent heart
seeks knowledge" (Prov 15:14). When Solomon prays for wisdom to help him be a good king, he asks for a "listening heart"
(1 Kgs 3:9). Insight and understanding originate in the heart;
in these instances, "mind" might be the best translation. The
heart is the very core of the human person, the center where
we are rooted. When Paul says that "the love of God has been
poured out in our hearts through the Holy Spirit who has been
given to us" (Rom 5:5), he is saying that the love which God
has for us, manifested in the Spirit, has been poured into the
very center of our persons from where it can (if we let it)
progressively radiate out and transform all areas of our lives.

The individual is a complex, rich, multifaceted phenomenon: "body," "soul," "breath," "heart," (and more, e.g.,
"blood," "bones," "bowels"). All these are different ways of
looking at the living unity which is the human person.[4]

Others

This living unity which is the human person does not, in
biblical thought, live alone. The individual always lives with

4. The basic work on these anthropological terms is H. W. Wolff,
Anthropology, 7–79. In addition, see H. J. Kraus, *Theology of the Psalms*
(Minneapolis: Abingdon, 1986) 138–50; L. Dunlop, *Patterns of Prayer
in the Psalms* (New York: Seabury, 1982) 1–12; R. B. Bjornard, "Beyond
Looks and Appearances," *TBT* 29 (1991) 133–38; J. L. McKenzie, "Aspects
of Old Testament Thought," *NJBC* 77:61-66.

others. The person cannot be separated out as some kind of "rugged individualist," but lives only immersed in community, surrounded by others.[5]

On the first level, one belongs to a "family;" this is a much larger group than our modern nuclear family (a fairly recent phenomenon). In addition to three or four generations together, the family embraced many relatives of varying degrees of proximity. A group of families made up a clan, and a group of clans made up a tribe. One ancient community of tribes was called "Israel" and formed a unity as Yahweh's people. Under the monarchy, Israel was a nation among all the nations of the earth.

Since individuals live rooted in these relationships, their actions are significant for the well-being of the community. Good, righteous actions build up the community, while wicked actions tear it down. "Through the blessing of the righteous the city is exalted, but through the mouth of the wicked it is overthrown" (Prov 11:11). "When the just are triumphant, there is great jubilation; but when the wicked gain preeminence, people hide" (Prov 28:12). The whole community has a stake in the behavior of the individual.

When in Scripture we meet an individual standing alone, this does not represent a normal situation. Often, it is the result of sin and brokenness. One may have been expelled from the community (e.g., Cain [Gen 4] or Achan [Josh 7:16-26]). The psalms of lament often speak of the pain of being alone (e.g., Ps 88:9, 19). At other times, individuals (e.g., Abraham, Moses, the prophets) may feel the pain of loneliness and separation, but this derives from their being chosen by God for special tasks. Their roles are intimately related to the welfare of the people as a whole.[6]

5. See B. Malina, "The Individual and the Community—Personality in the Social World of Early Christianity," *BTB* 9 (1979) 126–38; also H. W. Wolff, *Anthropology*, 214–16; J. L. McKenzie, "Aspects," *NJBC* 77:67-73; C. Westermann, *Elements of Old Testament Theology* (Atlanta: John Knox Press, 1982) 95.

6. H. W. Wolff, *Anthropology*, 216–22.

The World

We cannot, however, stop here. The individual and the community are themselves part of something larger: all of creation. As individuals we should not be isolated from other people; equally, we should not be isolated from natural creation. In the creation stories of Genesis 1 and 2, human beings are deeply rooted in the earth. The name *Adam* itself points to this; *adam* (human being) is taken from the *adamah* (the ground—Gen 2:7).

Just as human behavior affects other people, similarly it reaches to the very structure of creation itself. The flood story is a good example: "In the eyes of God, the earth was corrupt and full of lawlessness [Gen 6:11]. . . . All the fountains of the great abyss burst forth and the floodgates of the sky were opened [Gen 7:11]." The story begins by describing human sinfulness; lawlessness is everywhere. As a consequence, "the fountains of the great abyss burst forth." This is not a description of normal rain. The cosmic waters of chaos, which had been subdued and controlled in Genesis 1, return. The structure of the world collapses and returns to primordial chaos. Because of sin, even the earth falls apart. A similar idea appears in Isa 24:5-6: "The earth is polluted because of its inhabitants, who have transgressed laws, violated statutes, broken the ancient covenant. Therefore, a curse devours the earth, and its inhabitants pay for their guilt." The whole earth is utterly laid waste because its inhabitants have broken covenant with God.

A last example can be noted. In later biblical material, known as apocalyptic literature, it was common to list "signs of the end" (e.g., Matthew 24; Mark 13; Luke 21). Among the more common "signs" are these: families will be divided; nation will make war with nation; the sun will be darkened; the moon and stars will fall from the sky. Human disorder and cosmic disorder are mixed together. The logic is simple: we are all in this together.[7]

7. Another biblical example can be noted in the plagues in Egypt (see T. Fretheim, "The Plagues as Ecological Sign of Historical Disaster," *JBL* 110 (1991) 385–96, esp. 394–96). This point is the governing concept

God

Finally, all of this—the individual, the society, the natural world—exists not only in relationship to one another; all exist most deeply in relationship to God. (This is, in fact, the proper meaning of "creation.") Around, in, and through all these levels is God. A sense of God's closeness is pervasive throughout the biblical text. In earlier texts, God walks in the garden (Gen 3:8), sews garments (Gen 3:21), etc. As we move farther into the text, God becomes more removed, but the sense of intimacy with creation is maintained. Whether through dreams (Gen 28:10-22), messengers (Exod 3:2; Jdgs 13:3), the "name" (Deut 12:5), or the "glory" (Exod 40:34; Ezek 10), God continues to show care and concern for the people. Even in apocalyptic literature, where God seems far indeed, God continues to relate through dreams, visions, and heavenly messengers (angels), e.g., Daniel 7.

The sense of God's closeness in and through everything also is evident in the biblical view of miracle. For us, a miracle is something that so breaks natural laws that it must be attributed to God's direct intervention. The Bible knows a different approach. Since God is around and in the world, anything—natural phenomena, social event, or individual experience—can become the focus of God's presence and power. This then calls forth a response of wonder and marvel. For us, something which we cannot understand or explain which points to God is a miracle. For the Bible, *anything* that points to God is a miracle. God may break out anywhere; and the eyes of faith—recognizing this presence—marvel.[8]

In the biblical view, then, the individual person is located at the center of a series of relationships: other people, the natural world, God (see illustration 2.1, p. 26). To be human is to be interrelated. Further, these relationships are not sealed off

---

of T. Roszak, *Person/Planet: The Creative Disintegration of Industrial Society* (Garden City, N.Y.: Doubleday/Anchor Press, 1979). What is good for the planet is good for the person; what is bad for the person is bad for the planet.

   8. See M. Guinan, *The Pentateuch*, Message of Biblical Spirualilty 1 (Collegeville, Minn.: The Liturgical Press, 1990) 53–55; also, D. Senior, "Miracles of Jesus," *NJBC* 81:91-95.

from each other but are open and interconnected. An individual cannot be isolated but must be seen "in situ," immersed in the relationships which give and sustain life. The biblical view of human existence is wholistic, participatory, and dynamic.

The Basic Relationship: To God

Since being human means to exist deeply in relationships, do humans have any special role to play in and through these relationships? What is the human role within the world?

Image of God

In the first chapter of Genesis, we find our answer. Humans are not only part and parcel of the world, fully and deeply integrated into it; they are also the climax of God's creative activity, raised over creation as God's images. This is obviously an extremely important concept for spirituality.[9]

The first thing to note is that the Hebrews of the Bible were forbidden to make images of God (Exod 20:4; Deut 5:8). Why? We find a clue in the polemics against the idols which occur in various places of the Old Testament (e.g., Jer 10:1-11; Isa 40:18-20; 44:9-20; Dan 5:23; Ps 135:15-18). Over and over we meet the same charges: the idols of the nations are ineffectual, they can do nothing. They have eyes but see not; ears, but hear not; mouths, but cannot speak. They are dead. The living God of Israel can be imaged only by living beings who do what God does. God wants us humans to be that image.

What is involved in this? How do we go about it? Two things are essential. First, we must recognize and accept being an image. To be an image is to reflect another who comes first, another with whom we are tightly bound in relationship. This means we are not number one but number two. It involves a humble recognition on our part of creaturehood and of limi-

9. In what follows, I depend on the fuller discussion in *The Pentateuch*, 21–30. On image of God, see also H. W. Wolff, *Anthropology*, 159–65; J. Levenson, *Creation and the Persistence of Evil: The Jewish Drama of Divine Omnipotence* (San Francisco: Harper & Row, 1988) 111–17.

tation; a recognition that we, and all the relations to others and to the material world which make up our lives, exist only as gift. We are called into existence by, and are completely dependent upon the loving and life-giving word of God. Second, we must live out our imagehood. In the text, this is specified in two directions: (1) "Be fertile and multiply; fill the earth; and (2) subdue it—have dominion over the fish of the sea, the birds of the air, and all the living things that move on the earth" (Gen 1:28). In other words, we image God by doing exactly what we have just seen God doing. On the first three days of creation, God exercised dominion over the chaos (dark, windy, watery, formless) and brought out an ordered, harmonious, habitable universe. On the next three days (days 4, 5, and 6), God filled this universe with moving, living beings.

Each of these activities can be elucidated further. Since God's begetting life is done not through procreation (as in some ancient Near Eastern mythology) but through speaking the life-giving word (see also Deut 8:3; Amos 8:11), procreation, while an obvious way, cannot be the only way in which we image God's life-giving. It is manifested also in all our concerns for life and the quality of life.

The task of dominion appears, in words echoing our passage, in Psalm 8.[10] Dominion, ruling, subduing chaos is royal activity; in creating, God is exercising kingship (see further Psalms 93, 96–99). In royal contexts, two terms occur frequently to describe the task and obligation of the king to maintain an orderly realm in which other people and nature can live in right relationship. These terms are justice (*sedaqa*) and peace (*shalom*). Both point to integrity, wholeness, and harmony which are the opposite of chaos (see, e.g., Isa 9:5-6; 11:1-9; Ps 72). To share dominion, then, implies and includes working to build and maintain a universe marked by just, right relations and peaceful order. To be an image is to be a co-creator, sharing in God's royal activity of life-giving, justice-doing, and peace-making.

10. See T. F. Dailey, "Psalm 8 and Christian Anthropology," *TBT* 27 (1989) 242–44.

Failure of Imagehood

A question of prime importance is then: How do we humans image our God? The stories which follow immediately (Gen 2:4b–11:26) suggest that we do it rather poorly. Here we will focus on the first story, that of Adam and Eve (Gen 2–3). Adam is formed from the clay/dust of the ground and set up in charge of the garden (Gen 2:7, 15). This language also seems to have royal connotations; it was used to describe kings in Israel (1 Kgs 16:2). Eve is later formed from the side of Adam to be a partner like himself and to share responsibility for the garden (Gen 2:21-24). Their dominion, however, is not absolute but limited; they must not eat the fruit of the forbidden tree. The moment they do, they will die (Gen 2:16-17; 3:1-7). Together the man and woman violate God's command. They reject the limitations of creaturehood; they would rather be number one! The snake spells this out clearly, "You will be like gods!" (Gen 3:5).

What happens when the man and woman thus reject imagehood? All their relationships begin to come apart. They realize their nakedness and are ashamed (3:7); they hide from God (3:8); they argue and blame each other (3:9-12). Further, the relationship to animals, represented by the snake, is cursed (3:14), as is the relationship to the earth itself, which now yields life (its produce) only with great toil and difficulty (3:17). Finally, they will return to the dust from which they were taken (3:19). When we violate our relationship with God, all the other relations break down. When we reject imagehood and attempt to play God, we become death-giving, strife-making, and injustice-doing.[11]

Servant of Yahweh

Having failed miserably to live as images of God, humans need to be shown how. Their education begins with the call of Abraham and the examples of the other ancestors, particu-

11. We will have more to say about the meaning of death below in Chapter 4. For a broader discussion of the effects of the human attempt to play God, see D. E. Gowan, *When Man Becomes God: Humanism and Hybris in the Old Testament* (Pittsburgh: Pickwick Press, 1975).

larly Jacob and Joseph.[12] An important turning point is reached with the Exodus and the covenant at Sinai (Exod 1-15). The Hebrews are enslaved in hard labor in Egypt and cry out to God for deliverance (Exod 2:23). God hears their cry and sends Moses to represent them before Pharaoh and lead them out. Resistant at first, Pharaoh finally relents and allows the Hebrews to depart. Changing his mind, however, he pursues them and hems them in by the sea. The Hebrews are facing certain death at the hands of the Egyptians, but Moses urges them to be calm and have faith (Exod 14:13-14). Instead of death, Yahweh graces them with unexpected life. This event marks the foundation of Israel as a people.

The Israelites journey on to Sinai where they express their new relationship with Yahweh in the covenant.[13] Because of this, their behavior would be affected, and this in two areas. The first of these is their vertical relationship with God. Freed from the oppression of Egypt, the Hebrews now belong to Yahweh; they must live as Yahweh's special possession (Exod 19:4-6). Their deliverance was from the slavery of Egypt and for the service of Yahweh. "Let my people go so that they might serve me!" (Exod 4:23; 5:1; etc.). In effect, they become slaves of Yahweh (Lev 25:42). Israel's first duty was to be faithful to and worship only Yahweh. To worship any other god is idolatry.

The second area of obligation involves their horizontal relationship with others. Yahweh freed them from oppression in Egypt; the Sinai covenant revealed an intrinsic connection between the nature of Yahweh and the demands of social justice. How members of Israel treat each other will be a sign and manifestation of how serious they are in their worship of Yahweh. It would be a gross contradiction for Israel, freed from oppression by Yahweh, to become—in turn—oppressors of others.

In the years that followed, after their settlement in the land, Israel failed to live as servants of Yahweh and often and repeatedly violated these covenant obligations. It was the task of the

---

12. See my discussion of this in M. Guinan, *The Pentateuch*, 31-38.
13. Ibid., 62-66, 70-71.

prophets, through their criticism of Israel's empty worship and social abuses, either to call them back to their covenant fidelity or to announce God's punishment on their infideltiy.

Faith and Love

We find in the Old Testament two dominant models of what it means to be human: image of God and servant of Yahweh. One reflects what might be called a "high anthropology," the other, a "low anthropology." But they agree on seeing a twofold dimension to human moral life, what we might call a *passivity* and an *activity*. The first task is to receive, to accept imagehood, i.e., to accept our creaturehood and dependence on the creator God. The Sinai covenant commands that we recognize all of life as received from the redeeming God who frees us from oppression and who wants, in return, our sole and undivided worship and service. The second task is to live out our imagehood actively in and through all our relationships—through our concern for life, peace and justice. Sinai focuses this sharply through historical memory: "Do not oppress others (work for justice) because, remember, you were once oppressed in Egypt." The Sinai covenant is then another step in God's educating us in imagehood.

Later theology will speak of this twofold task in other terms. First, to accept imagehood and/or servanthood is an act of *faith*. By faith we recognize our complete dependence on God and therefore open ourselves to receive of God's fulness. We recognize that our whole lives are the gift of the redeeming God who delivers us from oppression and death. Second, to live this out in and through our other relationships is an act of *charity* or *love*. By charity, we work to express and restore, where broken, the life, justice, and peace that should characterize us in relation to others, to the world, and to God. If we really have faith in the God we say we do, it will be manifested in our lives; and conversely, the lives we live, the values we embody, will manifest who our God really is. The two are converse sides of the same coin and represent the challenge of being human before God.

The Human Role Fulfilled

As Christians, we find the fulfillment of what it means to be human in the person of Jesus Christ. Humans should relate to God as servants to their Lord (e.g., Matt 6:24; 10:24; 24:45-46; Lk 17:10). Jesus presents himself as a servant who washes the feet of others (John 13:1-20) and came in our midst "not to be served but to serve" (Mark 10:45; Matt 20:28). Though Jesus was "in the form of God, he emptied himself taking the form of a servant [slave]," (Phil 2:7). Unlike the Israel of old, Jesus remains faithful through all the temptations in the desert (Matt 4:1-11; Lk 4:1-13); he is the true Servant of Yahweh.

Likewise, Jesus is the "image of the invisible God" in whom all things are created. Through his death on the cross, he brings life, reconciliation and peace (Col 1:15-20). In fact, he himself is life (John 11:25), justice (1 Cor 1:30), and peace (Eph 2:11-22) in whom all things are made whole. The damage of Genesis 2–3 is healed. Full humanness is found in imitation of the life and teachings of Jesus and in sharing his death and resurrection through the gift of the Spirit.

The Other Relationships

We have seen that in the Bible, to be human means to exist at the center of relationships. We have seen further that the basic relationship which underlies all the others is the relationship to God. We can now ask about the other three relationships, namely, to the natural world, to other persons, and to oneself.

The first thing to note is that these other relationships are not optional. We cannot "not have" them. We may live them well or we may live them poorly, but live them we will. They are definitional of who we are as human. Secondly, inevitable as they may be, these relations are not central. As we have seen, the relationship with God is central and basic. To treat any other relation as central is to push God out; it is to fall into idolatry. When that happens, true faith and charity depart; idolatry leads to death and brokenness. Thirdly, while it does not take a lot of imagination to realize that material possessions, other people, and ourselves can and often do become idols, it does not follow from this that they are evil. We, by our sin, can turn them into idols; that does not make them demons. Throughout Christian history, movements have arisen to deny their value and worth (e.g., Gnosticism, Manichaeism, Jansenism), but they are all part of God's good creation.

Material Things. (1) Our need for material things should be obvious. We walk on the earth, breathe the air, need food and drink, shelter and clothing. Recent study has shown that other aspects of the material world around us—such as light, color, and sound—have a real but subtle affect on our health and behavior.[14] If we put these needs in the center of our lives, this is materialism; my value as a person comes from what I have, what I own. A subtle temptation, met at times by religious people, can be the opposite: I get my value from what I do not have. "I have less than. . . ." This is just materialism in reverse.

If our relation to things is ordered rightly, we recognize that our value comes not from our possessions but from being a creature of God. At times this is expressed in terms of being detached from things, but this is to view it from the negative side. The positive side points to a radical rooting or attachment of ourselves to God. This is often described as *"anawim* faith," the stance of the poor and humble before God. In addition, we are moved to respond to the material deprivation of others. Through our actions, we are called to put an end to situations and structures of need and oppression (Acts 2:42-47; 4:32-35).[15]

Other persons. (2) Likewise, our need for other persons needs no justification. From conception and birth on, our growth into whole and healthy persons depends on others.

14. See A. C. Hastings, J. Fadiman, J. S. Gordon, eds., *Health for the Whole Person* (Boulder, Colo.: Westview Press, 1980): article 18 (L. J. Kaslof, "The Therapeutic Use of Plants") 263–76; article 19 (H. L. Bonny, "Music and Sound in Health") 277–84; article 20 (P. C. Hughes, "The Use of Light and Color in Health") 285–99.

15. See further M. Guinan, *Gospel Poverty: Witness to the Risen Christ* (New York/Ramsey, N.J.: Paulist, 1981) 76–80.

We need acceptance, affection, and touch[16]; support, understanding, and love. As we grow, sexuality—an essential part of being human—enters into our relationships with others. Modern psychology confirms what we have seen in the biblical picture: to be excluded, rejected, alienated is an evil and destructive condition[17]

If our relation to others is ordered rightly, we can recognize the dignity and uniqueness of others; they will not be valued only as objects for our possession, control, or pleasure. Sexuality can be embraced as the gift of God that it is.[18] We will also be able to relate to and care for others as human beings just like ourselves. We can imitate Jesus who so often is presented as looking at others with compassion (e.g., Mark 1:41; 6:34; 8:2; Matt 14:14; Luke 7:13; 15:20) and then responding to their needs.

Ourselves. (3) And finally, we come to our relation to ourselves. To exist in the world is to have value and dignity. Hopefully, my existence in the world will make a difference for the better; the ability to make a difference is another way of saying "power." Because of the abuses so often connected with power, we often tend to shy away from the word; but, like material possessions and other persons, the unique power in the world that I am/you are is a good gift of God. Powerlessness, like material deprivation and human alienation, is an evil and has been recognized as the root of violence.[19]

If our relation to ourselves is ordered rightly, we will be able to accept ourselves as creatures of God, limited but raised up. Our sense of self and value will not depend on power that we have over others; we will be freed, rather, to use the power

16. See A. C. Hastings, et al., *Health*, article 14 (R. Frager, "Touch: Working with the Body") 209–25.

17. This negative type of aloneness should not be confused with solitude, an important, even essential, aspect of being human.

18. From the vast literature, two good places to begin would be J. B. Nelson, "Reuniting Sexuality and Spirituality," *The Christian Century* (Feb. 25, 1987) 187–90; E. E. and J. D. Whitehead, *A Sense of Sexuality* (New York: Doubleday, 1989).

19. See R. May, *Power and Innocence: A Search for the Sources of Violence* (New York: W. W. Norton, 1972) 19–45.

that we are in nuturing and integrating ways. We are called
to be instruments of God's power for life, peace, and justice
in the world.[20] Whatever Jesus was, he was not powerless; his
contemporaries noted how he spoke and taught "with
power/authority," (Matt 9:8; Mark 1:22, 27) and his deeds of
healing are called "acts of power" (Matt 11:20; Mark 6:5). Jesus
himself is called "the power of God" (1 Cor 1:24); and his disciples are sent out into the world to be his witnesses in and
by the power of the Spirit (Acts 1:8; 4:33).[21]

With all of these relationships the question is not, Material
things, other people, power: Yes or No? Good or Bad? (The
Christian answer is clearly, Yes, and Good.) Rather the question is, Material things, other people, power: with God or without God? With God, things are in order and we are on the road
to life and wholeness; without God, things are disordered and
we fall into brokenness and death. By our behavior we can
turn these good gifts into idols and then, like all idols, they
become destructive. The Christian corrective to misuse is not
nonuse but proper use.

In a recent book, Richard J. Foster discusses the problems
of *Money, Sex, and Power*[22] and offers as a counterbalance the
vows of simplicity, fidelity, and service. This is helpful, but
I would suggest further that these concerns can be related to
the traditional Christian virtues of poverty, chastity, and obedience.[23] With each of these we are dealing with the effect,
the overflow—as it were—of our life of humble faith in God

20. R. May distinguishes two kinds of negative power, power
over/against, and two kinds of positive power, power *with/for*; between
these is competitive power which is ambiguous. One can compete against
one's opponent or with one's partner (*Power and Innocence*, 105–13).
For an illuminating discussion of the power of God, see F. Baur, *Life in
Abundance*, 148–79.

21. See D. Senior, "Miracles of Jesus," *NJBC* 81:94; J. Fitzmyer, "Pauline Theology," *NJBC* 82:64.

22. R. J. Foster, *Money, Sex and Power: The Challenge of the Dis-
ciplined Life* (San Francisco: Harper & Row, 1985).

23. Members of religious orders who take public vows of poverty,
chastity, and obedience are living common Christian virtues within the
contexts of their particular community life and tradition.

and grateful love into all the areas of our lives. We receive the gifts of God only in and through all these relationships, and we live out our loving response likewise only in and through these relationships. If our relationship with God is central and in order, the seductive potential of our other relationships is held in check. Will we live as image, as servant of God? Will we respond to the call to be truly human before God?

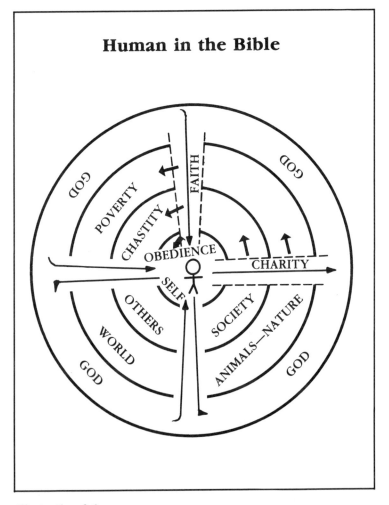

Illustration 2.1

Chapter 3

Am I Saved or Am I Blessed?

Each of us is created and called by God to be a unique embodiment of Christian spirituality in our world today. We do not, however, do this as isolated individuals. To be human is to live at the center of a series of relationships in and through which we experience our call by God, and in and through which we live out that call. The basic question is: Do we put the relationship with God at the center of our lives, or are we seduced by the goodness of the other relations into making them idols? In our lives and in our world, we can move toward life and wholeness or toward death and brokenness. Generally speaking, we can find ourselves in good situations or in bad situations, and these two situations correspond to two streams of biblical theology with their concomitant styles of spirituality.

Two Biblical Theologies

We will begin our study by looking at these dominant streams of biblical theology. One may respond, "Don't bother me with theology. I just want to know what I have to do. Let me go to church and say my prayers (or whatever)." Of course, if we want to do that we can, but let us be honest: theology and spirituality are closely interrelated. The lived Christian experience which is spirituality obviously comes first, but it then generates a theological position which in turn looks back at spirituality to evaluate and criticize it.[1] The theological dimen-

1. See the discussion in S. Schneiders, "Theology and Spirituality: Strangers, Rivals, or Partners?" *Horizons* 13 (1986) 270–73.

sion is present and operative even if we choose to ignore it; in the long run, though, it is healthier to recognize this and articulate it from the beginning.

Within biblical studies a consensus is growing that we find two dominant theological approaches, two continuing "trajectories."² These can be conveniently labelled *saving theology* and *blessing theology.* Saving theology (or salvation history) is certainly well known. It is found above all in the Old Testament in the accounts of how, in the Exodus, God saved Israel from the slavery of Egypt, covenanted with them at Sinai, guided them safely through the wilderness, and finally delivered to them the land of Canaan. In their critique of Israel's failures to live the covenant, the prophets appealed to these memories either to motivate Israel to repent or to provide the basis of judgment.

Blessing theology, on the other hand, is less familiar and is more scattered throughout the Old Testament.³ In a way, it is not just one approach, but three, each of which is distinct and capable of being studied independently; but in fact, the three do overlap and intertwine so that a certain unity emerges. The three in question are (1) creation theology (e.g., Gen 1–11; Ps 8, 104); (2) royal theology, centered on the Davidic traditions of Jerusalem (e.g., 2 Sam 7; Ps 72, 89); and (3) wisdom theology (e.g., Prov, Job, etc.). The interconnection of these three can be expressed in the affirmation, "The king, by ruling wisely, is in charge of the cosmic order (creation)."

In what follows, we will describe first saving theology and

2. Two articles by W. Brueggemann ("Trajectories in Old Testament Literature and the Sociology of Ancient Israel," *JBL* 98 (1979) 161–85; and "A Convergence in Recent Old Testament Theologies," *JSOT* 18 (1980) 2–18) survey and summarize these studies.

3. The work of C. Westermmann has been foundational in recovering the blessing theology. See especially *Blessing in the Bible and the Life of the Church* (Philadelphia: Fortress, 1978); *Elements of Old Testament Theology* (Atlanta: John Knox Press, 1982) 35–117; this is presented in condensed form in *What Does the Old Testament Say About God?* (Atlanta: John Knox Press, 1979) 25–52. See also the articles in M. Collins and D. Power, eds., *Blessing and Power* (Concilium 178; Edinburgh: T.& T. Clark Ltd., 1985).

then blessing theology. After that, we will say something about the interrelationship between the two.

Saving Theology

We can begin by asking, Where does saving theology originate? We are not asking where it begins in the biblical books, but rather where it begins in human life and history. It begins with the Hebrews enslaved in Egypt and in their experience of being helpless, oppressed, and powerless. They cry out to God in their distress (Exod 2:23) and God hears their cry. This starting point, not surprisingly, will affect how saving theology sees both God and human existence.

God is seen above all as Savior or Redeemer. "I am Yahweh, your God, who led you out of the land of Egypt" (Exod 20:2; Lev 22:31-33; Deut 13:6; etc.). This declaration becomes a summary of who God is for Israel. Having heard the cry of the Israelites, God intervenes in their history to set the slaves free. "With mighty hand and outstretched arm," God smites Pharaoh with the plagues; delivers Israel from certain death at the Sea; gives them food and drink in the wilderness (water from the rock [Exod 17:2-7]; manna [Exod 16]); protects them from enemies (e.g, Deut 25:17-19); brings them in and gives them the land of Canaan (Josh 24:11-13). All of these "signs and wonders" (e.g., Exod 10:1-2; Deut 6:21-22; Josh 24:17; Jer 32:20) are God's mighty deeds of salvation which form the basis of Israel's distinct identity as a people.

In this framework, what does it mean to be human? The saving theology finds expression in the covenant at Sinai. The Israelites had been slaves of Pharaoh, owing Pharaoh their "hard work/servitude" (Exod 1:13-14). Once saved from Pharaoh, they belong to Yahweh to whom they now owe "hard work/servitude." They were slaves of Pharaoh; they become slaves/servants of Yahweh (e.g., Lev 25:42).[4] As such they owe Yahweh alone their worship (Exod 20:2-3), and their behavior toward each other must express this. Yahweh is a God who freed from oppression and slavery; Israel must not op-

---

4. See my discussion of this in *The Pentateuch*. Message of Biblical Spirituality 1 (Collegeville, Minn: The Liturgical Press, 1990) 63, 70-71.

press or enslave others. We find a strong sense of social obligation. Why? "Remember, you yourselves were once slaves [aliens, oppressed] in the land of Egypt" (e.g., Exod 22:21; 23:9; Lev 19:34; Deut 15:1-11). What is the goal of saving theology? "Now, Israel, hear the statutes and decrees which I am teaching you to observe, that you may live. . . ." (Deut 4:1). Israel is saved from Egypt in order to live; but this is, in a way, life from the bottom up. The Hebrews had experienced oppression in Egypt and had faced certain death at the Sea. Yahweh gifts them with life. The covenant is given, with its obligations, to show them the way to life.

When we come to the New Testament, we can see that the saving theology of the Old Testament finds its fulfillment in Jesus. He is our Redeemer and Savior who frees us from the slavery of sin and death. He is the new Moses who gives us a new covenant in his blood (e.g., Matt 26:27-28) and a new covenant law (e.g., the Sermon on the Mount [Matt 5-7]; the Last Supper commandment [John 13:34]). Jesus also shows us what it means to be servant (e.g., John 13:15). The very name "Jesus" means, in Hebrew, "Yawheh saves."

Blessing Theology

We turn now to blessing theology and ask the same questions of it: Where does blessing theology originate? It begins with kings or queens in Jerusalem; with counsellors, advisors, and sages in the royal court who are consulted for their wisdom; with parents and elders in a family or tribe. All of these are people in positions of power and authority, people in charge who can make a difference. This affects how blessing theology views both God and human existence.

In blessing theology—with its threefold weave—God is the King who, by his rule, establishes cosmic order (Psalms 93, 96–99); God is the Creator/Maker of the world and all that is in it (Gen 1); God creates through and with wisdom, personified as the Wisdom Woman who continues to be present and active in the universe (e.g., Prov 8:22-31). Here too God performs "signs and wonders," but these are now the deeds of creation and constant care (e.g., Job 5:9; 9:10; 37:14; Ps 107:24; 136:4). God is also present in and through everyday lives and relationships. The Joseph Story (Gen 37–50) provides a parade example. We read of Joseph and his brothers; of his problems in Egypt with Potiphar's wife; of his rise to power and authority over Egypt—second only to Pharaoh. But in and through all of this, it is God whose purposes are being worked out (Gen 45:4-8; 50:20). In blessing theology, God does not intervene from without but works from within the natural and social orders.

What does it mean to be human within this theological context? Blessing theology finds ultimate expression in the covenant with David who is chosen to be king for Yahweh. To be human is to share this kingship; it is to be created in the royal image of God (Gen 1:26-28; Ps 8).[5] This implies, as we saw in chapter two, that we first accept our dependence on God (e.g., David too must obey Yahweh or be punished, 2 Sam 7:14; Ps 89:31-33). We are limited, and wise living is to recognize and live within these limits. The beginning of wisdom is fear of the Lord (e.g., Prov 1:7; Job 28:28). A strong sense of social (and cosmic!) obligation appears. Do not oppress the poor. Why? Whoever oppresses the poor blasphemes the Maker (Prov 14:31; 17:5; 29:13; Job 29:12-20). The appeal here is not to a common historical memory, but to the fact that poor and rich, weak and powerful alike have a common Creator. The concerns for peace and justice are in fact primary obligations of kingship (e.g., Ps 72).

What is the goal of blessing theology? "Long life is in her (Wisdom's) right hand . . . she is a tree of life to those who grasp her. . ." (Prov 3:16-18). Again, the goal is life; in a way, that is the only goal. But in blessing theology, it is life from the top down. The kings, queens, counselors, and sages were blessed, and the covenant with David is given to remind them

5. In the saving covenant theology, the king is pulled down to be just one of the people (Deut 17:14-15), while in the blessing covenant theology, all people are pulled up into kingship. Both of these represent a "democritizing" tendency, but they move in opposite directions. See J. Levenson, *Creation and the Persistence of Evil: The Jewish Drama of Divine Omnipotence* (San Francisco: Harper & Row, 1988) 114–16.

of their obligations to be instruments of life, peace, and justice, not only for Israel but for the world.
When we come to the New Testament, blessing theology also finds its fulfillment in Jesus. He is the son of David who preaches and brings in the Kingdom of God. His Lordship will ultimately be acknowledged by all (Phil 2:9-11). He is the wisdom of God (1 Cor 1:24); in him, all things are created in the heavens and on the earth (Col 1:15-20). Also, he shows us what it means to be image of God (Col 1:15). The title "Christ," which is a Greek translation of the Hebrew "Messiah," means primarily "anointed king." So when we say "Jesus Christ," we affirm both the saving and the blessing theological streams brought together and united in his person, teaching, life and work.[6]

The Interconnection Between Saving and Blessing Theology

It is clear that these are two very different theological orientations, rooted in different kinds of experiences. It is also clear that they are both present extensively in the Scriptures and cannot be ignored or discarded. It is the one God, Yahweh, who is both the Creator and the Redeemer (e.g., Ps 136). As different as they are, they do share certain things in common: (1) They share the anthropology we discussed in chapter two. To be human is to be immersed in multilevelled relationships. When these break down and come apart, one needs saving; when they are healthy and alive, one is blessed. (2) They share a common faith in God, a recognition that we come from and depend on God, Creator and Redeemer, in all of our lives. (3) They share a sense of awe and marvel before the wonderous works of God, the mighty acts of deliverance or the wonders of creation all around us. (4) They share a strong sense of social responsibility, for putting an end to oppression and for being instruments of God's justice in the world.[7]

6. D. DiDomizio, "Christological Paradigms in Spirituality," *Chicago Studies* 24 (1985) 87–96, argues that the two images of Christ the Liberator (i.e., saving) and the Cosmic Christ (i.e., blessing), with their mutual interaction, hold much promise for the future.
7. For some other common elements, see J. Goldingay, *Theological Diversity and the Authority of the Old Testament* (Grand Rapids: Wm. B. Eerdman's, 1987) 215–16.

How, finally, should these two theological traditions be related? When we come to this question we enter an area where debate among scholars continues and is far from resolved. Some would accept one as normative and reject the other as an aberration (something the Old Testament itself obviously did not do). The Mosaic tradition is more frequently kept and the Davidic rejected; or one can hold the two together but subordinate one to the other, the Davidic to the Mosaic, or vice-versa, the Mosaic to the Davidic. Or should they be seen as thoroughly dialectic?[8]

Below, I will suggest a possible way of relating these in the light of spirituality. Here, we can just warn against separating them too sharply. In a real sense, "redemption can be spoken of as an act of creation, and creation as God's first act of salvation."[9] The relation between them can be pointed to in four statements: (1) the world God redeems is the world of God's creation; (2) the world God created is a world that needed to be redeemed; (3) human beings are redeemed to live again their created life before God; and (4) the redeemed humanity still looks for a final act of redemption/re-creation.[10]

Two Spiritualities

It has already become apparent that these two theological traditions would be related to two rather different styles of spirituality. We turn now to sketch some characteristics—and perhaps dangers—of each of these spiritualities. In doing this, we will overstate the case a bit so as to clarify each spirituality in contrast to the other. The results may sound a bit artificial,

8. J. Goldingay has an extended discussion of this in *Diversity*, 200–239.

9. J. Goldingay, *Diversity*, 216. C. W. Mitchell, *The Meaning of BRK "To Bless" in the Old Testament* (Atlanta: Scholars Press, 1987) 23–24, 177–79, also warns against too sharp a distinction between deliverance and blessing.

10. These four statements are cited from J. Goldingay who also gives a discussion of each one, *Diversity*, 216–39; on the interrelation of saving and blessing, see G. Landes, "Creation and Liberation," *Creation and the Old Testament,* ed. B. Anderson (Philadelphia: Fortress, 1984) 135–51; T. Fretheim, "The Reclamation of Creation," *Int* 45 (1991) 354–65.

but afterwards we will try to balance this by saying something about their interrelationship.

A Saving Spirituality

A saving spirituality, obviously, is marked by a strong sense of being "saved." "Have you been saved?" No uncertainty is possible because "being saved" is a dramatic conversion experience. We are going along in our everday lives, and, suddenly, from "out there," we are knocked off our horses. This turning point is often described as "being born again." We can date it; there is a clear *before* and *after.* Our first birth does not count; the past is rejected. Often, the conversion experience will lead to baptism, but in those churches who practice infant baptism, the first baptism is of little value. It is the later baptism "in the Spirit" that counts. Descriptions of this kind of conversion are not uncommon in certain "lives of the saints:" the early life of the saint was filled with sin and selfishness; but then, something happened! and from that time on, the saint was changed. If it is discussed at all, growth in faith is seen as taking place in the same manner as coming to faith in the first place: it occurs at breaking points, or crises of disjunction. The old collapses and the new is born.[11] "Real" Christians are those who have been born again, who have been saved.

This kind of language, popular in fundamentalist Protestantism, was not common in Roman Catholicism until after Vatican Council II with the growth of the charismatic movement and its strong experiential style. However, we did have something like it in our approach to religious orders. Religious were supposed to have died to their past (often symbolized in investiture ceremonies by the candidates' lying on the floor and being covered with a black pall). When they "rose," they received a new name as a sign of their new life. Some theologians even developed theories that profession in a religious

11. This view has been well articulated by W. Brueggemann, "The Exodus as Israel's Articulation of Faith Development," in *Hope In History* (Atlanta: John Knox Press, 1987) 7–26. I would, however, disagree with seeing this as *the* biblical view. See below, footnote 14.

order had the effects of a second baptism! And religious were often regarded by the laity as the "real" Christians.

"Amazing grace, how sweet the sound, that saved a wretch like me." To be human is to be a wretch, weak and helpless, filled with sin and selfishness. Some fundamentalist groups even proclaim a doctrine of total human depravity. While hardly representing mainstream orthodoxy, this does point to a problem. Such a "low" anthropology can lead to a great suspicion of oneself and one's gifts. "God has given me real musical talent, but since I might be tempted to pride, I will throw this in the garbage and devote myself to teaching history!" Such distrust of self is often manifested in a cautious, conservative style which is afraid to take risks in life. Finally, such a stress is conducive to bad self-image and low self-esteem, a condition closely connected with addictive behaviors.[12] This can be very disempowering; one might be moved to pray, in the spirit of Psalm 22:7 (or Job 25:6; Isa 41:14), "I am not human but a worthless worm." It is possible, however, that the worm may turn: "I am not worthless; I count! I have dignity and integrity." In the words of the old slogan, "I'm lovable; God don't make junk."

Given such a sense of self, with its concomitant sense of the world around as filled with sin and evil, saving spirituality tends to view the Church as a bastion against the dangerous world. Entering through the door of the conversion experience, the saved are now safe. Much more time is spent "within" in expressly religious activity: prayer, church meetings, and functions with like-minded people. Here another danger can be noted: sectarianism. We can see this already in the

12. "The first core belief of the addict is, I am basically a bad, unworthy person," P. Carnes, *The Sexual Addiction* (Minneapolis, Minn.: CompCare Publishing, 1983) 72–73. He further affirms, "co-addicts grow up in families in which their self-worth is constantly in jeopardy. Feelings of inadequacy and failure parallel the addict's sense of unworthiness," (p. 108). See A. W. Schaef, *When Society is an Addict* (San Francisco: Harper & Row, 1987); G. C. May, *Addiction and Grace* (San Francisco: HarperCollins, 1988). It is not surprising that extreme fundamentalism has been approached as an addiction; see Fundamentalists Anonymous, P.O. Box 20324, Greely Sq. Sta., New York, N.Y. 10001.

Mosaic covenant theology. Who did God save out of Egypt? Canaanites? Moabites? Hittites? No. God saved *us*. A big temptation is to help God decide who is and is not saved, and, not unsurprisingly, those who are saved come out sounding a lot like us. We are saved . . . and you are not!

The combination of a view of the self and the world as weak and filled with sin together with an emotional experience of being saved by a God who intervenes strongly from outside, produces a view of authority as strong and external. We look outside for guidance and security. What does the pope say? the priest? the religious superior? or the Bible?[13] And, as noted in chapter one, we can be tempted to give away the responsibility for our lives in exchange for security. One's view of ministry in the Church will obviously be affected, as will one's view of spiritual direction. The spiritual director is an authority whose guidance must be obeyed. As a reflection of the strong, external view of God, authority in the Church has a decidedly masculine, even "macho," tone.

A favorite image used in saving spirituality is that of light. I am in a dark room, stumbling and groping, when suddenly someone (from outside) turns on the switch! My eyes hurt; I blink and squint. The change is dramatic, exciting, and challenging. I see everything all at once. I "have seen the light!"

A Blessing Spirituality

A blessing spirituality does not stress "being saved." Instead, we find in it a pervasive sense of God's presence in, through, and around our lives. There are moments of closeness and warmth and moments of weakness and sin, but no big, dramatic turning points. Our first birth is enough; our first baptism is enough. The problem is: do we live it out? A more sacramental view of the world is in evidence. Descriptions of this kind of experience also appear in the "lives of the saints:" 'Saint So-and-so showed early signs of holiness; he took a vow of celibacy at the age of three and abstained from his mother's

13. This last is particularly insidious because the Bible does not *say* anything; it says what someone (Jerry Falwell? Jimmy Swaggart?) says it says. There is no such thing as an uninterpreted Bible.

milk on Monday, Wednesday, and Friday." God's grace was present and operative from the beginning. Growth in faith is gradual and developmental, occuring in interaction with our everyday lives and experience.[14]

This perspective also affects our view of religious life. Instead of a special or new way of being Christian, it is but one way among many of living out the common call of baptism. While this is not the only factor involved, it can help us understand why some religious do not take a new "religious" name, or, if they already have one, choose to go back to their baptismal names. Religious life is a living out of baptism.

Grace is still amazing, but it is experienced in a very different way. To be human is to be blessed by grace as image of God. We are capable, in charge, and trusted by God to be stewards of creation and society; we are called to live life creatively and not be afraid of risks. Such a "high" anthropology can lead to pride and smugness. We can go too far and violate the limits of creaturehood. If things go too well, it is easy to forget their ultimate source in God (see Deut 8:6; Prov 30:9; Hos 13:6) and take credit ourselves. Such a situation is conducive to neurotic behavior. "Every neurotic at bottom is loathe to recognize limitations. . . ."[15] As Sam Keen has observed, we would rather be a "miserable god than a satisfied human."[16] It is possible, however, that the god may come down from the pedestal and say, "I am not responsible for all; I am not alone." The extreme of saving spirituality sees humans as worthless worms; that of blessing spirituality, as gods (Gen 3:5). Neither extreme can accept just being human with its dignity and humility.

Blessing spirituality does not view the Church as a bastion against the world. Rather, it is more the setting for the Chris-

14. The existence of this "counterpoint" to a saving view of faith development is acknowledged by W. Brueggemann, *Hope in History,* but is relegated to a footnote (no. 57 on p. 117). It deserves much more serious consideration than that.

15. K. Horney, *Neurosis and Human Growth* (New York: W. W. Norton & Co., 1950) 36.

16. S. Keen, *Apology for Wonder* (San Francisco: Harper & Row, 1964) 147.

tian community to gather to focus on and celebrate God's presence and activity, a presence and activity also to be met in more diffuse fashion in the world (see Illustration 3.1, p. 39).[17] The world and the Church are alike places of sinfulness and places of grace. For this reason less time may be spent in expressly religious activity. "I pray while I'm taking the bus to work; while I'm walking in the park; while I'm listening to music or watching television!" To the blessed person, the saved person seems to be talking about Jesus all the time; to the saved person, the blessed person seems totally secular. If the danger of saving spirituality is sectarianism, the danger of blessing spirituality is excessive ecumenism. The particularity of Christian revelation can be washed out and disappear into some vague, cosmic, good feeling.

In the context of blessing, how is authority viewed? It is found within each one of us. We have our heredity, gifts, talents, and experiences. We are responsible to put these at the service of God's Kingdom. Through our sharing we hopefully can bear witness to the manifold activity and presence of the Spirit in our world. There is legitimate religious authority "out there," but it should not take away, much less trample over, the uniqueness that each one of us is. The view of ministry is much more tentative, shared, and collegial. Spiritual direction is seen more as a process of accompaniment, of sharing the spiritual journey. Since God nourishes, sustains, and acts through the regularities of nature (e.g., the Wisdom Woman), the way is open for more feminine (as well as healthier masculine) language and styles of leadership.[18]

Blessing spirituality can also talk of seeing the light. We are in the dark of night, and soon the sun, on its regular path through creation, begins to rise. There is a glow on the east-

17. These two theological/spiritual traditions clearly have implications for the question of the Church's relationship to culture and the issue of inculturation. See A. Dulles, "The Emerging World Church and the Pluralism of Cultures," in *The Reshaping of Catholicism* (San Francisco: Harper & Row, 1988) 34–50; P. Schineller, *A Handbook on Inculturation* (New York/Mahwah, N.J.: Paulist, 1990).

18. R. A. Jensen, "Human Experience and the Blessing/Saving God," *WW* 1 (1981) 237.

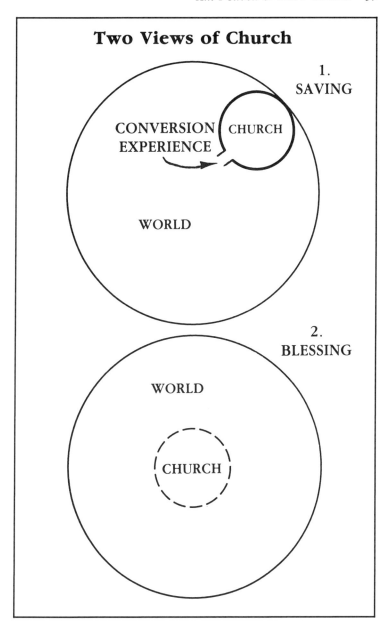

Illustration 3.1

ern horizon, and gradually, little by little, the room is illumi-
nated until it is filled with light. The purpose and goal is to
live in the light, but different kinds of experiences can lead
us to that goal.

The Interconnection Between Saving and Blessing Spirituality

Having looked at the two theological traditions of saving
and blessing and then suggesting some possible areas in which
they might be manifested in spirituality, we can now make
some comments on their interrelationship. Three things seem
worth noting:

(1) It is probably obvious that we have strongly overstressed
the saving tradition. The roots of this are not hard to identify.
The controversies of the Reformation and the post-Reforma-
tion period were focussed on such issues as sin, salvation,
justification, and grace. The twin movements of Puritanism and
Jansenism, with their negative views of the world and human
nature, have influenced us all in one way or another. While
taking their starting points in the Bible, they ignored other
balancing traditions and ended up with rather distorted doc-
trines. Following shortly after these, the European Enlighten-
ment and the Industrial Revolution marginalized the Church
more and more; it is no wonder that Christians felt themselves
besieged in a progressively hostile world.

(2) The saving tradition needs to be balanced, and, as we
have seen, there is ample biblical basis on which to do this.
We need both saving and blessing; the answer to the title of
this chapter—"Am I Saved or Am I Blessed?"—is certainly,
"Yes." It is possible to go too far in either direction. Fundamentalist Christianity, either Protestant or Roman Catholic,
would seem to err in the direction of the saving tradition;
charismatic Christianity leans in this direction also and needs
to be watchful. Certain types of "New Age" Christianity may
err in the direction of the blessing tradition.[19] The saving tra-

19. It has been suggested that Matthew Fox and his creation-centered
spirituality err in this way. Among his many works, see *Original Blessing* (Santa Fe, N.Mex.: Bear & Co., 1983); *Creation Spirituality: Liberating Gifts for the People of the Earth* (San Francisco: Harper, 1991). I

dition needs a sense of dignity and worth; the blessing tradition, a sense of humility, weakness, and limits. Neither alone adequately represents the biblical tradition.

We might attempt to correlate these two traditions with social, cultural settings. Thus, it might be suggested, the American culture with its optimism, abundance, and sense of power would be more open to the blessing tradition, while Third World cultures with their suffering and oppressive systems would more likely be receptive to the saving tradition. However, ironically, in the "blessed" American culture, fundamentalist churches with their extreme saving emphasis are very popular and apparently growing at a good pace; on the other hand, many "saving" Third World countries with their predominant agrarian economies are more in tune with the natural growth and oneness of creation represented by the blessing view.

Walter Brueggemann has tried to be a little more precise. The blessing trajectory (he tends to emphasize its royal character) is most likely to be lodged in university contexts rather than communities of faith and have an inherent bias toward social conservatism. The saving (liberation) trajectory is more likely to be lodged in a confessing community and have a bias toward social radicalness.[20] Unfortunately, this perspective does not prove itself in the concrete either. It is the "confessing communities" with the strongest focus on "being saved" which are most socially conservative and lack concern for peace and justice; while the forces for radical change are more often seen as "university radicals" who are out of step with society. Nicaragua under the Sandanistas would be a case in point, where the majority of the clergy and simple people (confessing communities?) are not terribly enthusaistic about the liberation theologians who are more supportive of the goverment. In times of social and political conflict, the certainties

---

would make just two general observations: (1) he surely has his finger on some important and neglected areas of the Catholic Christian tradition; and (2) his treatment and use of Scripture is not always adequate.

20. W. Brueggemann, "Trajectories," 184–85.

and securities of saving theology can be very attractive.[21] Also, the blessing tradition with its view of humans as image of God may be much more empowering of individuals in moving toward social change. Social and cultural reality would seem to be sufficiently complex to make generalizations shaky; but even with these generalizations we must still keep in mind that individuals within a given culture may differ from it quite a bit in their spiritual styles.

Personally and individually, each one of us is usually more at home with one style than the other. The reasons for this are surely varied, but personality plays an important role. The saving style of spirituality would find echoes in a conflict type of personality which feels caught in constant, on-going struggles with forces both within the self and without in society. The theories deveoped by Sigmund Freud, Henry Murray, and Otto Rank would be of this type. The blessing style, on the other hand, would find echoes in fulfillment or actualization types of personality which stress inner strength and resources. This would be reflected in theories such as those of Carl Rogers and Abraham Maslow.[22]

Of course, people, like societies and cultures, have a way of not fitting exactly into any theories; even the most "saved" person has good days, and the most "blessed," bad days; but whichever tradition speaks most to us, we need to keep a hold on the other so we do not lose focus or balance. The writer and humorist, E. B. White has said, "If the world were merely seductive, that would be easy. If it were merely challenging, that would be no problem. But I arise in the morning torn between the desire to improve or save the world, and a desire

21. See the discussion of this by P. Lernoux, *People of God* (New York: Penguin Books, 1989) 365–405. She notes the success of the traditional churches on p. 390. A similar observation is made by the journalist C. Krauss, *Inside Central America: Its People, Politics, and History* (New York: Summit Books, 1991) 166.

22. I am indebted to social psychologist Dr. Rosemarie Anderson for seeing the connection between the Mosaic/Davidic covenant styles and types of personality theory (from a personal communication with me, Dec. 7, 1982). See further, S. R. Maddi, *Personality Theories: A Comparative Analysis* (Homewood, Ill.: Dorsey Press, 1980).

to enjoy or savor the world; this makes it hard to plan the day."[23] The words of the Jewish Hasidic master, Simha Bunan of Pzhyshka are also appropriate: "Everyone must have two pockets so that he can reach into the one or the other according to his needs. In his right pocket are to be the words: 'For my sake the earth was created,' and in his left: 'I am earth and ashes.' "[24] Claus Westermann highlights a significant passage in the book of Joshua[25]: "On that same day, after the Passover on which they ate of the produce of the land, the manna ceased. No longer was there manna for the Israelites, who that year ate of the yield of the land of Canaan" (Josh 5:12). We have here the transition between two kinds of bread: (1) manna, the saving bread God provided in the wilderness which the Israelites had just to gather up, and (2) the produce of the land which depends on God's constant, creative blessing activity, but also demands human participation (planting, harvesting, cooking). An important spiritual question then might be, "What kind of bread do we need?"[26]

(3) So we have two separate spiritual traditions and it appears we need them both. Can we then say that they are *separate but equal,* that they should be balanced fifty-fifty on the teeter-totter of our lives? Perhaps not. An example from the field of medicine may clarify the question. The medicine that we are most familiar with can be called *crisis medicine.* We get in trouble and need help. We catch the flu, get pneumonia, break a leg and call the doctor! The doctor intervenes from outside with pills or treatment to set us right. Recently, however, another approach to medicine known by the broad designation *holistic medicine,* is attracting attention.[27] Its concern

23. Somewhere along the line this quote was given to me by a student but unfortunately, without the exact reference.

24. M. Buber, *Tales of the Hasidim: The Late Masters* (New York: Schocken Books, 1948) 2:249–50.

25. C. Westermann, *Elements,* 106; *What Does the Old Testament Say About God?,* 46.

26. I first heard Westermann's insight applied spiritually this way by W. Brueggemann, "The Bailey Lectures," American Baptist Seminary of the West, Berkeley, Calif., 1979.

27. See A. C. Hastings, J. Fadiman, J. S. Gordon, eds., *Health for the*

is not with crises but with trying to prevent them by maximizing health. It asks questions such as, What about your diet? Do you get enough exercise? Do you have too much stress in your life? How's your emotional health? Given these descriptions of health care, it may be argued that both approaches are necessary. If we get hit by a car and have broken bones, it is not very helpful to have someone run up to us, lying on the pavement, and ask, "Pardon me, but do you eat whole grain cereals and jog three times a week?" But is health just a question of not being sick or injured? Where do we get our vision of what "health" really means?

Saving spirituality is like crisis medicine and blessing like holistic medicine. We need both, but not in the same ways. We and the world we live in are a mixture of death and life, sin and grace. We are weak and sinful, and our world is broken and incomplete. Suffering and injustice are real. We do need to be saved. But we are also graced and empowered as images of God to go forth into the world to make a difference. Once "saved," where do we go from there? The rich biblical picture of life, peace, and justice derived from the blessing tradition provides the context for our response. It lies always ahead of us and stands in judgment on any partial, incomplete realization in the here and now. It is an eschatological vision that sends us out now to share in Jesus' work of the Kingdom but which comes to its fulness only in the future as God's complete gift.[28]

The relationship between these two approaches is one of dynamic interaction. As we follow Jesus down the road of our lives, in our spiritual automobiles as it were, sometimes we are humming along the highway on cruise control. At other times we may be broken down on the side of the road and need to call the great AAA in the sky. We have both a broad windshield to help us see where we are going, and rear view

---

Whole Person: A Complete Guide to Holistic Medicine (Boulder, Colo.: Westview Press, 1980). This volume is based on a report prepared for the National Institute of Mental Health.

28. For a discussion of this dynamic from a theological point of view, see Z. Hayes, *Visions of a Future: A Study of Christian Eschatology* (Wilmington, Del.: Michael Glazier Press, 1989) 126–53.

mirrors to help us see where we have been. Jesus did come to save us, to redeem us, to heal us; but he also came that we might have life, life in abundance (John 10:10). As we grow into our vision of fulness, may we never settle for less.

Chapter 4

The Goal: Life, Peace, Justice

When it was asked earlier, What does it mean to be human in the Bible, we saw that the Bible does not give us a simple, one sentence definition. The living human is a rich and complex phenomenon, and the Bible circles around this phenomenon, seeing first one aspect, then another, then another. We noted that this has been termed *stereometric thinking.* When we come now to the question, What is the goal of our life in the world, to what is God calling all of us?, we should not be surprised to find a similar situation. The Bible uses a number of images, comparisons, metaphors, to speak about this: e.g., we are in darkness, and God calls us to light; we are oppressed, and God saves us. Three closely related images are especially important: God calls us to life, peace, and justice. We have mentioned these terms before but since our modern English usage and the biblical usage are by no means identical, we need to examine them in more detail. We will begin by looking at each within the Old Testament before turning to the New.

The Old Testament

Life (Ḥayyim)

When we ask the question about life or death (Is So-and-So dead or alive?), our approach is fairly straightforward. Whether we look at heartbeats or brain wave patterns, we are dealing with a physical problem involving a physical answer. While it includes this, the biblical view is much broader and richer.

To begin to gain a sense of what *life* means in the Bible, we can look at its concept of death. We touched on this earlier when we spoke of the failure of imagehood. Created in the image of God, men and women are charged to accept that imagehood and live it out in and through all of their relationships (Gen 1:26-28). The stories that follow in Genesis are meant to show us how this is done: Adam and Eve (Gen 2–3); Cain and Abel (Gen 4); Noah and the Flood (Gen 6–9); the Tower of Babel (Gen 11). In each story, there is failure and sin; in each story, a punishment follows.[1]

Adam and Eve eat of the forbidden tree (2:16-17; 3:1-7); Cain arrogates to himself power over life and kills his brother Abel (4:8); the generation of the flood fills the earth with wickedness and lawlessness (6:5, 11). The Hebrew word translated "lawlessness" or "violence" (*ḥamas*) is often usd to describe social injustice (e.g., Mic 6:10-12). Finally, the people of Shinar (in Babylonia) want to make for themselves a great tower and a great name (11:4). In each story, the sin is basically the same: humans reject imagehood and prefer to play God (Gen 3:5). And what happens then?

In each story, the sin is followed by a punishment: for Adam and Eve, it is basically death (2:17; 3:19); Cain is made to wander alone over the earth (4:12); the flood comes destroying the sinful generation (7:6-8, 14); at the tower, the people are scattered, and their languages confused. All of these punishments are covered by the biblical concept of *death*. Death is not just the last breath at the end of life; it is more. It is the breaking and collapse of all our relationships at all levels. Death is not just a moment at the end but a whole realm of brokenness that pervades our lives.

In discussing the Adam and Eve story earlier, we noted how each of the relationships (to God, to others, to the world, to self) began to come apart, but we missed something else. Adam and Eve had been told that at the very moment they eat of the tree, they will die (2:17). They eat, but go on living for a long time—Adam for 930 years (5:5)! The fact is that the very moment they ate, they did die—the process began. All their relationships started to come apart. The stories that follow illustrate various aspects of the realm of death. Since Cain can-

1. See my discussion of this in *The Pentateuch*. Message of Biblical Spirituality 1 (Collegeville, Minn.: The Liturgical Press, 1990) 26–31.

not live in peace with his brother, he must wander alone, out
of community (4:12). Human injustice which brings the flood,
breaks down and destroys not only the social order but also
the cosmic order. With profound insight, the tower of Babel
story recognizes that the scattering of people and their inabil-
ity to communicate with each other is likewise a manifestation of death. We are made for life, for *communion* with. In
its place, we beget death.

One further dimension of death needs to be noted. Even
though God is depicted as intervening and pronouncing a sentence, the punishment of death is not arbitrary and imposed
from the outside. It flows from and expresses the inner nature of sin. We humans are created from the life-giving word
of God and breathe with the breath (spirit) of God. When we
reject God, we turn our backs on the source of our life; we
reach out and cut off our air supply. And what is the cutting
off of life but death? When we do this, all the relationships
which make up life begin coming apart. Sin is simultaneously
both murder and suicide. Death is an expression, a manifestation, of what sin truly is.

Whatever death might be, there is one thing it is not: it is
not the last word. God created the world and humans for life,
and God's purpose will prevail. Each of the four stories just
noted ends with a sign of hope or promise. Eve is named the
"mother of all the living" (3:20), and God makes garments to
cover their shame (3:21); Cain fears that he too will be killed,
but God puts a mark on him for protection (4:15); Noah and
his family and some animals survive the flood and are the
source of new life on earth (8:21-22); the tower of Babel finds
its "happy ending" in the call of Abraham with its repeated
promise of blessing (12:1-4). As curse is the power of death,
blessing is the power of life, and God's will for blessing and
life will prevail.

Life characterizes God. In contrast to the gods of the nations who are dead, Yahweh is the living God (Jer 10:1-10;
Deut 5:26; Josh 3:10). In solemn oaths, the Israelite would
swear, "As God/Yahweh lives. . ." (2 Sam 2:27; 1 Kgs 1:29),
and Yahweh would swear, "By my life. . ." (Num 14:21, 28).
God is the source, the fountain of life (Ps 36:10). For the Is-

raelites, the blood which flowed through the body was seen as the seat of life; since life came from God and was sacred, they were forbidden to eat any meat with the blood still in it (Gen 9:4-5; Lev 17:11-12). The value of one's life does not depend on who one is or what one does; all life is sacred because it is a gift of the living God. Life is experienced in a special way in the sanctuary, the temple, which can at times be designated simply "the land of the living."[2]

Blessing, as the power of life, appears prominently in the book of Deuteronomy which speaks often of the consequences which flow from covenant fidelity.[3] *Life* includes *longevity*—a long life (belief in an afterlife appears only very late in the Old Testament: 4:40; 5:15; 22:7) in the *land* (6:10, 18; 8:7-10) marked by the abundant *fertility* (life) of fields, flocks, and family (7:12-13; 28:3-6) which makes for *prosperity* and *affluence* (6:12; 8:7-13), to be shared with great *joy* (12:18; 16:15; 26:11). Life, then, is more than just breathing air; it refers to the concrete fulness of all our relationships. Biblical life is co-life.

Peace (Shalom)

When we speak of peace, we tend to understand it primarily as an absence of war or strife; it is defined in a negative way. It is "not" something. In the Bible *shalom* (the root occurs almost five hundred times) is a positive term which describes a state or condition of being whole, intact, entire, complete. For example, if one has made a vow to the Lord, it is conceived as being incomplete until one has brought it to fulness (*shillem*) by the performance of whatever was promised.[4]

2. See M. L. Barre, "'rs [h]hyym—'The Land of the Living'," *JSOT* 41 (1988) 37–59. For further discussion of the biblical concept of life, see H. J. Kraus, *Theology of the Psalms* (Minneapolis, Minn.: Abingdon, 1986) 162–68; G. Gerleman, "hjh-leben," *THAT*, 1:549–57; G. von Rad, " 'Righteousness' and 'Life' in the Cultic Language of the Psalms," in *The Problem of the Hexateuch and Other Essays* (Edinburgh and London: Oliver & Boyd, 1965) 243–66.

3. See M. Guinan, *The Pentateuch*, 113–14.

4. See G. Gerleman, "šlm-genug haben," *THAT* 2:919–35.

If we are ill, our bodies do not have their proper wholeness; in some way they are coming apart. Thus the psalmist laments, "There is no health in my flesh . . . no wholeness (*shalom*) in my bones" (Ps 38:4). Physical health is peace. We may be torn apart by worry and anxiety, but when trusting in Yahweh, "as soon as I lie down, I fall peacefully asleep . . ." (Ps 4:9). Mental health is peace.[5] Socially, peace can describe the condition in which strife and conflict between peoples is absent (e.g., Judg 4:17). Peace also describes human relationships with animals, and when the soil yields abundant crops, that too is peace (Lev 26:6-10; Zech 8:13). Peace is overall fulness, as when Abraham is promised that he will die at a ripe old age, "in peace" (Gen 15:15). Joseph is sent to inquire after the general well-being of his brothers (Gen 37:14). *Peace* can be used as both a greeting (Judg 6:23; Ezra 5:7) and a farewell (Exod 4:18). Peace is a term which covers all our relationships on all levels.

Peace occurs in two important contexts. The first is that of covenant. A covenant, in the ancient world, was a social/political instrument to bring together in unity two peoples, clans, tribes, nations who were separated either as strangers or enemies (a thin line for the ancients). Thus the whole purpose of a covenant was to establish peace.[6] There had been strife between Isaac and Abimelech, a Philistine king. They made a covenant (Gen 26:28) and departed from each other in peace (Gen 26:30-31). As a reward for his zeal, Yahweh made with Phineas "my covenant, peace" (Num 25:12). Consoling the exiles in Babylon, Yahweh assured them "my covenant of peace will not be shaken" (Isa 54:10). Looking to Israel's restoration in the land, Ezekiel assured them, "I will make a covenant of peace with them" (Ezek 34:25).

The second important context in which peace occurs is that of kingship. In a special way, the king is responsible for peace in the realm. In Isaiah's famous Davidic oracle, "a child is born

5. On the connection between healing and peace (and blessing), see C. Westermann, "Salvation and Healing in the Community: The Old Testament Understanding," *International Review of Mission* 6 (1972) 9–19, esp. p. 10.

6. See M. Guinan, *The Pentateuch*, 58–62.

to us, a son is given to us; . . . they name him Prince of Peace. His dominion is vast and forever peaceful" (Isa 9:5-6). While the word is not used, the concept of peace certainly underlies the vision of the wolf lying down with the lamb, and the baby playing with snakes (Isa 11:6-9). The royal responsibility for peace is a recurring theme in Psalm 72. Interestingly, two of David's sons, Absalom and Solomon, have names which include the Hebrew word *shalom*. And we can recall that in Gen 1:26-28 and Psalm 8, all humans are drawn up into kingship. To be human is to share responsibility for peace.

Finally, peace is with God and comes to us from God. Yahweh is the one who "makes peace" (Isa 45:7). Peace for David comes from Yahweh (literally, "from-with Yahweh," 1 Kgs 2:33). Yahweh blesses the people with peace (Ps 29:11; Num 6:24-26). These last two references show the connection between blessing (life) and the gift of peace.[7]

Justice (*Ṣedaqa*)

"There is absolutely no concept in the Old Testament with so central a significance for all the relationships of human life as that of *ṣedaqa*."[8] When we think of justice in the Old Testament, the role of the prophets comes immediately to mind (e.g., Amos 5:7-13; 8:4-6; Jer 7:1-10), but it would be a mistake to think that this is a distinguishing characteristic of the prophets. It is found in the Law (e.g., Exod 22:21; 23:9; Lev 19:34; Deut 10:18; 14:28), in wisdom (Prov 14:31; 17:5; 29:14), in the Psalms (72:1-4; 97:2, 6), and in royal contexts (Isa 9:6; 11:3-5). The concern for justice pervades the Old Testament.

For us, justice usually connotes social behavior which accords with some abstract ethical or legal norm. One is just if one conforms to this norm. This is not the way the Old Testa-

7. See J. I. Durham, "Shalom and the Presence of God," in *Proclamation and Presence*, J. I. Durham & J. R. Porter, eds. (Richmond, Va.: John Knox Press, 1970) 272–93.

8. G. von Rad, *Old Testament Theology* (New York: Harper & Row, 1962) 1:370. For other discussions of *ṣedaqa* in the Bible, see K. Koch, "ṣdq-gemeinschaftreu/heilvoll sein," *THAT* 2:507–30; L. G. Perdue, "Cosmology and the Social Order in the Wisdom Tradition," in *The Sage*

ment approaches the question. Justice is a term of concrete
relationships. We live enmeshed in relationships and each of
these brings with it certain claims on our behavior. To be just
is to live these relationships faithfully.

Yahweh is the Just One (Jer 23:6). Justice is the foundation
of God's throne (Ps 97:2); justice has been wrought in Jacob
(Ps 99:4); Yahweh is in the midst of Israel as Justice (Zeph 3:5).
Yahweh's fidelity to Israel was manifested in the mighty acts
of salvation which are called "deeds of justice" (Jdgs 5:11; Mic
6:5). But Yahweh's justice operates not only in the arena of
history; the whole realm of nature is likewise involved. God
gives "the early rain in justice" (Joel 2:23), and fertility of the
soil is a manifestation of God's justice (Ps 65:6-14; 85:12-14).

Israel is Yahweh's people and must, in response, live justly.
This appears in the two main relationships of covenant responsibility: to God and to others. Abraham's faithfulness to
God is reckoned as justice (Gen 15:6); Israel is to offer just
sacrifices to Yahweh (Ps 4:2; 51:21; Deut 33:19; Mal 3:3). To
go after idols or false gods is to violate their relation with Yahweh. They are also to treat each other justly (Exod 23:7; Lev
19:15). Above all, there must be justice in the courts and at
the city gates where cases are heard; judges should beware of
bribery which distorts the giving of just decisions (Deut 16:18-
20; Amos 5:7, 10-13). If one is faithful to God with right worship and to others in and through social behavior, then one
is just and will live (Ezek 18:5-9). Fidelity to the covenant is
also manifested in the way we treat the natural environment
(Deut 20:19-20) and animals (Deut 22:6-7; 25:4).

The monarchy is a special place where the concern for justice comes into focus. The king is responsible for peace in the
realm; he is also responsible for justice. Just as Yahweh's throne
is established on justice (Ps 89:15; 97:2; 99:4), so too must that
of the human king, Yahweh's representative. "Kings have a
horror of wrongdoing, for by justice the throne endures" (Prov
16:12); "Kindness and piety safeguard the king, and he upholds
his throne by justice" (Prov 20:28). A similar thought in different words is found in Proverbs 29:14: "If a king is zealous for

in Israel and the Ancient Near East, (J. G. Gammie & L. G. Perdue, eds.
(Winona Lake, Ind: Eisenbrauns, 1990) 457–78, esp. 458–59.

the rights of the poor, his throne stands firm forever." The king is to be endowed with God's justice and judgment, a justice manifested especially in the concern of the king for the poor, the weak, and the helpless (Ps 72).[9] David is said to have reigned over the people justly (2 Sam 8:15); and again we recall that to be human in the image of God is to be raised up to share God's royal dominion.

Justice in the Bible is a rich term of relationship. Yahweh is Justice, and Yahweh's deeds of justice are manifested in historical events as well as the rhythms of nature. As Yahweh's special people, we are called to be just in the way we worship only Yahweh and in the way we treat each other. The king and those in authority have a special responsibility in this regard. In the light of this, we can see the inadequacy, from a biblical point of view, of separating worship of God and social justice. In the last century, it was not uncommon to read that the prophets rejected worship of God in favor of social justice; a more recent variation would argue that we should first do justice and only after that go and worship.[10] The two are flip sides of the same coin and both are included as part of *ṣedaqa*.

It is also inadequate to set the Mosaic covenant (with a concern for justice) over against the Davidic, royal covenant (with a concern for order).[11] Both covenants have a strong sense of justice; likewise both can be (and were) violated. If a situation

9. See M. Guinan, *Gospel Poverty: Witness to the Risen Christ* (New York/Ramsey, N.J.: Paulist, 1981) 26–31; N. Lohfink, *Option for the Poor* (Berkeley, Calif.: Bibal Press, 1987) 16–25.

10. For example, J. Miranda, *Marx and the Bible* (New York: Orbis, 1974) 58.

11. W. Brueggemann, *The Prophetic Imagination* (Philadelphia: Fortress, 1978) and many of his more recent writings. What he describes as "royal consciousness" indeed represents a serious threat to justice; to identify this, however, with Israel's royal covenant tradition is something else. One beginning indication: over two-thirds of the occurrences of the root *sdq* occur in texts deriving from that Jerusalem theological complex; see K. Koch, *THAT* 2:511. Also, the Hebrew word for *justice* is *ṣedaqa*; the Hebrew word for *order* is *ṣedaqa*. The royal theology is concerned for the order which equals justice; if the royal *order* violates justice, then it is also violates the royal theology.

of injustice exists, there is a double problem. Some people are oppressed because others are oppressors. The Mosaic covenant records the cry of the oppressed for justice; the Davidic preserves the challenge to kings and those in power to estab lish justice as true representatives of Yahweh's rule. Both cove- nant traditions have strong and important contributions to make to the cause of justice.

Guides on the Way

If we are to live and act as God's images, as Yahweh's ser- vants/slaves—being instruments of life, peace, and justice in the world—we will need some help, some guides. There are many possibilites for failure, for breaking down, along the way. We have in the Bible two main guides; the first of these, rooted in the Mosaic saving tradition, is the Torah.

Torah, which literally means "instruction," has most often been translated *law,* but this is not very helpful. Torah basi- cally refers to Israel's covenant story with Yahweh. It tells what God has first done for Israel, and then how Israel is to respond. There are indeed laws and commandments, but these exist only in a narrative framework which provides the basis for them. This covenant instruction was passed on orally at first in the context of Israel's worship, but then, over time, it began to be written down. At the end of this process we have the Torah, i.e., the first five books of the Old Testament—the Pentateuch. A word better than Law to help us understand and appreciate Israel's Torah might be *revelation,* for it is in the Torah that we learn who God is and what God is about, and how we are to live in grateful response.[12]

"If you obey the commandments of the Lord, your God, . . . you will live . . . and the Lord, your God, will bless you" (Deut 30:16). "Now, Israel, hear the statutes and decrees which I am teaching you to observe, that you may live" (Deut 4:1). "Keep, then, my statutes and decrees, for the man who car- ries them out will find life through them" (Lev 18:5). "Justice and justice alone shall be your aim that you may have life" (Deut 16:20). "If you would hearken to my commandments,

---

12. See M. Guinan, *The Pentateuch,* 123–28.

your peace would be like a river and your justice like the waves
of the sea" (Isa 48:18); on the other hand, for those who are
not faithful, "There is no peace for the wicked, says the LORD"
(Isa 48:22; 57:21). However, "Those who love your *torah* have
great peace" (Ps 119:165). These few representative citations
suffice to show that fidelity to the Torah is the road to life,
peace, and justice.

The second guide, rooted in the blessing tradition, is
wisdom. Wisdom is an elusive term which has a range of meanings; but in general, we can speak of it in terms of two quali-
ties. On the one hand, wisdom describes the human search for
knowledge and understanding. It depends on and speaks from
experience (e.g., Prov 24:20-24); it is found in the everyday
happenings of our lives and our reflection on them. The beginning of wisdom is fear of the Lord (i.e., obedient faith; Prov
1:7; 9:10; Job 28:28), and throughout our search, we are called
to recognize the creaturely limitations of our understanding
(e.g., Prov 16:1-3). On the other hand, wisdom comes from
God and is personified as the Wisdom Woman who mediates
between God and the world of creation. She calls to us at the
crossroads of our lives, in creation and in our experience (Prov
1:20-33; 8:1-36). We are urged to seek wisdom, and Wisdom
from God comes seeking us.[13]

Wisdom cries out, "He who finds me, finds life . . . all
who hate me love death" (Prov 8:35-36). "With me are en-
during wealth and *ṣedaqa*," (Prov 8:18). "Long life is in her
right hand, in her left are riches and honor; her ways are pleas-
ant ways, and all her paths are peace; she is a tree of life to
those who grasp her, and they are happy (blessed) who hold
her fast" (Prov 3:16-18). "In the path of justice there is
life . . ." (Prov 12:28). We should follow the teachings of wisdom, "For many days, and years of life, and peace will they
bring you" (Prov 3:2). Wisdom will watch over and guard us
on the path to life, peace, and justice (Proverbs 2).

13. For good discussions of wisdom, see R. E. Murphy, *The Tree of
Life: An Exploration of Biblical Wisdom Literature* (New York: Doubleday, 1990), and K. O'Connor, *The Wisdom Literature.* Message of Biblical Spirituality 5 (Collegeville, Minn.: Liturgical Press, 1988).

In the writings of later Judaism, shortly before the time of Christ, these two traditions came together. Wisdom continues to be found in all of creation and throughout all our experience, but it comes to a clear, sharp focus in the Torah Wisdom goes forth from God, covers the earth, but pitches her tent in Israel and is found in the Torah (Psalm 19; Ben Sira 24:1-22). Echoing the words of Proverbs 3 quoted above, wisdom is "the book of the precepts of God, the law that endures forever; all who cling to her will live, but those will die who forsake her" (Bar 4:1). In the late, apocalyptic book of Daniel, when we get some of the first clear indications of belief in an afterlife, it is the wise who will share in this life (Dan 12:2-3), and one of the charateristics of the wise is their fidelity to God and the Torah (e.g., Dan 1).

God has created us and the world for life, peace, and justice, and we have the Torah and Wisdom to guide us along the right path. If instead we have death-brokenness, injustice, and no peace, the Bible does not look primarily to social, economic, or political causes. These are symptoms of something deeper. The root cause is religious: idolatry! We have forsaken the God of life.

The New Testament

Life

By his ministry, Jesus brings life. He enters the house of Jairus and restores his dead daughter to life (Mark 5:21-43; Matt 9:18-26; Luke 8:40-56). He encounters the funeral procession of the only son of a widow of Naim. Jesus raises the son and gives him back to his mother (Luke 7:11-17). Jesus' good friend, Lazarus, has died, and by the time that Jesus and his disciples arrive, Lazarus has been three days in the tomb. Jesus calls him forth (John 11). In ancient Palestine, the dead were laid out in the house, then carried outside the city to the cemetery, where they were buried. In the three miracles of restoration to life, one in the house, one on the road, and one at the grave, it is as if Jesus is setting up signposts of hope all along the road of death. Life—not death—is the last word.

Jesus not only restores to life; he himself *is* Life. This is a theme that recurs throughout the Gospel of John: "What came to be through him was life" (1:4); "the water I shall give will become . . . a spring of water welling up to eternal life" (4:14). Jesus is the "bread of life" (6:48), "the light of life" (8:12), "the resurrection and the life" (11:25), and "the way, the truth, and the life" (14:6).

Peace

At Jesus' birth, the angelic chorus announces "peace on earth" (Luke 2:14). Throughout his ministry, when he brings forgiveness and healing, he often concludes, "Your faith has saved you; go in peace" (e.g., Luke 7:50; 8:48). In fact, Jesus' miracles of healing (*shalom*) are signs that God's kingdom of peace is already being realized.[14] Peace is Jesus' gift to his disciples on the night before he died: "Peace I leave with you, my peace I give to you" (John 14:27); and this gift is confirmed on the evening of the first Easter: "Peace be with you," and he breathed on them and said, "Receive the Holy Spirit" (John 20:19-20). The peace which Jesus brings, however, is not an easy peace. Faithful proclamation of God's kingdom of peace meets resistance and rejection; in this sense, paradoxically, the bringer of peace brings not peace but a sword (Matt 10:34; Luke 12:51).[15] The whole work of Jesus is characterized as "reconciling all things . . . making peace by the blood of his cross" (Col 1:20).

Not only does Jesus bring peace (forgiveness, healing, reconciliation), he himself *is* Peace: "For he is our peace, he who made both (i.e., Jew and Gentile) one and broke down the dividing wall of enmity, through his flesh . . . that he might create in himself one new person in place of the two, thus establishing peace, and might reconcile both with God, in one body, through the cross, putting that enmity to death by it. He came and preached peace to you who were far off

14. D. Senior, "The Miracles of Jesus," *NJBC* 81:112.

15. J. P. Meier, *Matthew*. New Testament Message 3 (Collegeville, Minn.: The Liturgical Press, 1980) 113; see also, B. Viviano, "The Gospel of Matthew," *NJBC* 42:71; R. J. Karris, "The Gospel of Luke," *NJBC* 43:137.

and peace to those who were near, for through him we both have access in one Spirit to the Father" (Eph 2:14-18). All the barriers of religion, society, and sex have been broken down in him (Gal 3:28); wholeness is restored.

Justice

As Messiah-King, Jesus brings a kingdom of peace; he brings one also of justice. The beginning of his ministry is marked by the proclamation, "The Spirit of the Lord is upon me . . ./ to bring glad tidings to the poor./ He has sent me to proclaim liberty to captives/ and recovery of sight to the blind,/ to let the oppressed go free,/ and to proclaim a year acceptable to the Lord" (Luke 4:18-19, citing Isa 61:1-2). When John the Baptist sends disciples to question Jesus, he replies, "Report to John what you hear and see . . ." (Matt 11:5; Luke 7:22); and he pronounces blessings on the poor, the afflicted, and the hungry (Luke 6:20-21). Jesus' mission and teaching is good news for the poor and the oppressed because the advent of God's kingdom means that these unjust conditions are at an end.[16]

Jesus not only brings justice, he *is* Justice. He is the Just One (Acts 3:14; 7:52) who comes to fulfill all justice (Matt 3:15). Jesus became justice for our sakes (1 Cor 1:30).

Guides on the Way

The two Old Testament guides, Torah and Wisdom, also find their fullness in Jesus. Jesus presents himself as the fulfillment of the Torah (Matt 5:17). This is not a question merely of finding a particular verse here and there in the Torah which can then be applied to Christ. As the Torah in Judaism embodies the revelation of God, so does Jesus in Christianity. In Jesus we see who God is and what God is about, and we see how we are to live in grateful response.[17]

Jesus is, further, "the power of God and the wisdom of God"; he "became for us wisdom from God" (1 Cor 1:24, 30). Jesus is understood in terms of wisdom throughout the New Testament. The earliest Christological hymns (e.g., Col 1:15-

---

16. See my *Gospel Poverty*, 58–65.
17. See *The Pentateuch*, 128–29.

20; Eph 2:14-16), for example, reflect the cosmic dimensions of wisdom; Matthew's Gospel presents Jesus as Wisdom come to earth and calling disciples, and "wisdom is vindicated by her works" (Matt 11:19). The Gospel of John presents an especially developed Christology drawing on wisdom themes. Just as wisdom is with God before all creation, comes forth from God, and pitches her tent in Israel (Ben Sira 24), so too with Jesus, who comes forth from God and "pitches his tent among us" (John 1:1-14).[18]

The Life of the Christian

The fullness of the Kingdom achieved in Jesus has yet to be worked out on earth. While it has "already" begun, it is "not yet" completely realized. We Christians, followers of Christ, live in this in-between time, living and breathing with his Spirit and are called to continue Christ's work in the world. Through baptism, we share Christ's death and begin to live in newness of life; just as he died to sin, so we should think of ourselves as dead to sin and alive in Christ (Rom 6:4-11). We are not to live under the dominion of sin, weakness, and the flesh, but rather under the Spirit of life (Rom 8:1-17).

"The concern of the Spirit is life and peace" (Rom 8:6). Christians are sent into the world to be bearers of Christ's peace. "Blessed are the peacemakers, for they shall be called children of God" (Matt 5:9). Paul frequently exhorts Christians to be instruments of peace (e.g., Rom 12:18-19; 14:19; 1 Cor 14:33); and peace is one of the fruits of the Spirit (Gal 5:22).

Closely connected with peace is justice. The kingdom of God is a matter of justice, peace, and joy in the Spirit (Rom 14:17), and Christians are urged to pursue justice, faith, love, and peace (2 Tim 2:22). The fruit of justice is sown in peace (James 3:18). By their lives, Christians are to put an end to hunger and oppression (Matt 25:31-46). A good model can be seen in Zacchaeus (Luke 19:1-10) who first hears the call of Jesus;

18. On Jesus as Wisdom, see the summary with references in K. O'Connor, *Wisdom Literature*, 185–92; J. M. Reese, "Christ as Wisdom Incarnate: Wiser than Solomon, Loftier than Lady Wisdom," *BTB* 11 (1981) 44–47.

in the light of this, he recognizes his own contribution to injustice and moves to change this. "Behold, half of my possessions, Lord, I shall give to the poor, and if I have extorted anything from anyone [a very likely possibility for a tax collector] I shall repay it four times over" (Luke 19:8).

Throughout the New Testament we note the close connection of life, peace, and justice with the Spirit of God. If we truly live by and in that Spirit, our lives should be transformed by these concerns. Life, peace, and justice are not intended for the few, or for just some groups or political parties. They are of the essense of our human life before God in Jesus.

Chapter 5

Let Our Prayer Come to You

To be human is to be related to the self, to others, to the world, and to God. The relation which is most basic, which stands at the center of our lives is the one which overflows and affects all the others; the relation to God should be that center. If this is so, we are on the road to life, peace, and justice. A very important element in keeping our lives moving in this direction is prayer.

From at least the eighth century, prayer has been understood as "the lifting of the mind and heart to God" (from the Syrian, Arabic writer, St. John of Damascus, d. ca. 750). To help us do this, we are fed from the great sources of Christian prayer, the table of the Scriptures and the table of the Eucharist.[1] Over the centuries, however, both of these became less and less accessible to most Christians, a situation that would come to a head in the sixteenth-century Reformation.

Sometime earlier, spiritual writers began to discuss and propose more explicit methods of prayer or spiritual exercises which could help people pray more effectively. While not the first, certainly the most famous of these is *The Spiritual Exercises* of Ignatius of Loyola. Later writers along this line would include Peter of Alcantara, Theresa of Avila, John of the Cross, Francis de Sales, and J. J. Olier.

An important shift occurred with Vatican Council II. While the roots of the modern biblical and liturgical movements go back into the eighteenth and nineteenth centuries, they came to fruition in the work of the Vatican II Council. The recovery and renewal of these traditional sources of nourishment could not but effect Christian prayer.

1. Thomas a Kempis, *The Imitation of Christ*, 4.11.4.

In the light of what we have seen so far from biblical spirituality, we can now ask, "What can we learn from the Scriptures about prayer?" This is obviously a large question, one which we cannot exhaust here,[2] but perhaps we can begin to gain some insights if we look at the Book of Psalms. One can approach this collection of Israel's liturgical hymns from a variety of angles, e.g., historical, literary, theological. Here we would approach the Psalms as a "school of prayer." What can we learn from them of how the biblical people prayed? More specifically, we can ask four questions: (1) *Who Prays?*; (2) *To Whom?*; (3) *How?*; and (4) *From Where?* The first three we can treat somewhat briefly, but the fourth will need more development.

Who Prays?

When we ask "Who prays?" we are asking about the *I* of the Psalms, but not in the sense of "Is the *I* the king? a priest? a cultic prophet?" Rather, we are asking the question of basic anthropology, and it is a question we addressed at length in chapter two. To pray, in the Psalms, involves more than just the mind, the will, the intelligence (i.e., the powers of the spiritual soul); it involves the whole person, body and soul, in all its dimensions.

"In the entire Bible, Old and New Testaments, there is hardly any group of texts so well suited for the study of aspects of anthropology as the Psalms."[3] It is here especially that we find the multifaceted self (body, soul [throat], spirit [breath], heart, etc.) embedded in relationships. Whether these go well or badly, it is from this context that the psalmist prays.

To Whom?

If our first question had to do with the *I* of the psalms, the second has to do with the *Thou*. Obviously, the psalmist prays

2. For a somewhat fuller introduction see R. E. Clements, *In Spirit and In Truth: Insights from Biblical Prayer* (Atlanta, Ga.: John Knox Press, 1985).

3. H. J. Kraus, *The Theology of the Psalms* (Minneapolis, Minn.: Abingdon Press, 1986) 143.

to Yahweh, the God of Israel. With this God Israel has a history. Yahweh is the Creator of the whole universe and all that is in it. In time, Yahweh chose Israel as a special people and saved them from the oppression and slavery of Egypt. We discussed these in chapter three. With this God Israel has a relationship which is brought to expression in the covenant, whether Mosaic or Davidic. This God is close to Israel and cares for Israel.

How?

On the basis of this history, this relationship and this closeness, the psalmist prays to God. The language of prayer is thus dialogical. However, this has a further impact on the language of prayer. Most of our everyday speech is discursive or descriptive, dealing with facts of our regular experience. When we come to our deep, personal relationships—our loves, our hopes, our visions—this way of speaking is not adequate. Everyday descriptive language breaks down, and we take recourse in the language of poetry. We are trying to express something which, in a real sense, is more than language can express; it is *personal* language. This continues to be true when we wish to speak out of the deepest relationship of our lives, the one to God. The language of the Psalms, then, is poetry, and poetry which abounds in rich and diverse images and comparisons applied both to the *Thou,* God (e.g., a Rock [Psalm 92:15], a Fortress [Psalm 94:22], a Shepherd [Psalm 23:1]) and to the *I,* the self (e.g., water poured out . . . heart melting like wax . . . throat dried up like baked clay [Ps 22:15-16]).[4]

From Where?

Living as human individuals immersed in a series of relationships, we can experience these relationships either as alive

4. Most introductions to the Psalms have some discussion of Hebrew poetry. Among others see R. Alter, *The Art of Hebrew Poetry* (New York: Basic Books, 1985) 111–36; J. Kselman, "Psalms: Poetry at its Best," *Pastoral Music* 8/6 (Aug–Sept 1984) 6–7; J. Craghan, *The Psalms: Prayers for the Ups, Downs and In-Betweens of Life* (Collegeville, Minn.: The Liturgical Press, 1985) 19–20.

and growing more and more into union, or as coming apart and breaking down. In the former case, we are in the realm of life; in the latter, that of death. Out of experiences of life and blessing, we praise; out of experiences of death, we lament and call on God to save us.

Praise

The English word *psalms* comes from the Greek and means "songs sung to musical accompaniment." The title of the book in Hebrew is *tehillim*, which means *praises.* (From the same root we have *Hallelu-Yah* = *Praise-Yahweh*.) Thus, the whole book is put under the heading praises. But what exactly do we mean by praise? Often we equate it with thanksgiving, with saying Thank You to God. While this is a part of praise, it is not the first or most important element.

The first thing to note about praise is that it is connected closely with life. "It is not the dead who praise the LORD, nor those who go down into silence" (Ps 115:17; also 6:5; 30:9; 88:10-11). Death is characterized by lack of praise; on the other hand, life manifests itself in praise. There cannot be true life without praise of God. "Praise becomes the most elementary 'token of being alive' that exists."[5] "Praising God and being a living creature belong together in the Old Testament."[6]

Instead of offering a definition, let me illustrate the meaning of praise with an example.[7] When my youngest nephew was two-and-a-half years old, I gave him for Christmas a purple teddy bear. As he began to open it, his eyes lit up, he tore off the rest of the wrapping and ran back and forth between his

5. G. von Rad, *Old Testament Theology* (New York: Harper & Row, 1962) 1:370.

6. C. Westermann, *Elements of Old Testament Theology* (Atlanta, Ga.: John Knox Press, 1982) 158; *What does the Old Testament say about God?* (Atlanta, Ga.: John Knox Press, 1979) 66.

7. See M. Guinan, "The Ecstacy of Praise; the Depths of Lament," *Pastoral Music* 8/1 (Oct–Nov 1983) 17–19; *The Pentateuch*. Message of Biblical Spirituality 1 (Collegeville, Minn.: Liturgical Press, 1990) 55–56; P. D. Miller, " 'Enthroned on the Praises of Israel:' The Praise of God in Old Testament Theology," *Int* 39 (1985) 5–19 (reprinted in *Interpreting the Psalms* (Philadelphia: Fortress Press, 1986) 64–78).

parents saying, "Mama, papa, Look! Uncle Mike gave me a purple teddy bear!" Only later, with parental direction, did he come and say "Thank you." If he had not, I doubt I would have noticed; I had something better than thanks.

Children have to be taught to say Thank you; they do not have to be taught to praise. "Mama, papa, Look! Uncle Mike gave me a purple teddy bear!" is praise. It is a spontaneous, religious Wow!; it calls to others; it focuses on the giver and the gift. The self is present only as the recipient (grammatically, the indirect object). In thanksgiving, the self becomes the subject of the sentence: *I* thank you. Praise is the spontaneous response to the giftedness in life and the giftedness of life, and it focuses on the Giver and the gift. "Praise is the joy of existence turned toward God."[8]

This simple illustration contains all the key elements of praise. Psalm 117, the shortest psalm, is representative:

> Praise the LORD, all you nations;
> > glorify him, all you people.
> For steadfast is his kindness to us,
> > and the fidelity of the LORD endures forever.

The psalmist calls to others. In the grandest praise, the call goes out not only to other Israelites, not only to all nations, but also to all of creation (e.g., Ps 148). Here, as it were, the chorus is at its fullest. All of creation comes to voice and expression when humans, the culmination of creation, praise God. The experience of life involves the experience of healthy, growing relationships on all their levels.

After the call to others, a reason is given: *for, because*. Sometimes, as here in Psalm 117, the reason is a more general description of God and God's attributes. At other times, more concrete acts of deliverance are recalled: "I sought the LORD and he answered me . . . when the afflicted cried out, the LORD heard," (Ps 34:5; also, e.g., Ps 30). The first type has been called descriptive praise (or traditionally, *hymns*), the second, narrative praise (or traditionally, *individual thanksgiv-*

8. C. Westermann, *Elements*, 93.

ing); but in both, the Giver and the gift are proclaimed.[9]

This proclamation of the Giver and the gift is important for another reason. When we do this, we are remembering what God has done for us, and memory is an essential part of our lives. What is it that memory does? From time to time we hear in the media of persons being found with complete amnesia (literally: *no-memory*). They do not know their names or their families; where they came from or where they are going; how they got where they are. Memory gives us identity; it tells us who we are, where we are from and where we are going.

When speaking in chapter three of the dangers of a blessing spirituality, we noted that we who are blessed can be tempted to forget the source of our blessings and mistake ourselves for God. We forget that we are an image and violate the limits of creaturehood. This danger is clearly recognized in the Scriptures: in the Law (e.g., Deut 8:6), the Prophets (e.g., Hos 13:6), and the Writings (Prov 30:9). Praise helps us to keep ourselves in focus and to guard against these abuses. Psalm 8 contains perhaps the strongest statement of the elevated royal role of humans: You have made them little less than the angels (or, than God!) and crowned them with glory and honor! But this psalm also begins and ends with praise (8:2, 12). When the power of imagehood begins and ends with praise, we remember who we are and how we are to live. Praise is a corrective to the possible excesses of a blessing spirituality.

Praise is, then, a response to the giftedness of life, a response that focuses on the Giver and the gift and shares this with others. It is prayed out of joy, of strength, of happiness, and of blessedness. It is a corrective to pride, arrogance, and the abuse of power because in praise we recognize our dependence and our creaturehood. The words of Abraham Heschel are appropriate here: "Prayer is our humble answer to the inconceivable surprise of living."[10]

---

9. These terms are those of C. Westermann, *Elements*, 159–67; see the discussion of them in P. D. Miller, "Enthroned," 10–16.

10. A. Heschel, *Quest for God: Studies in Prayer and Symbolism* (New York: Crossroad, 1982, 1954) 5.

Lament

It does not take much imagination to realize that our lives are not all joy, happiness, and strength. At times we experience just the opposite. We know brokenness and pain, alienation and confusion, doubt and the absence of God; in these situations we groan and cry out for saving (Exod 2:23). At these times we lament, "My God, my God, why have you forsaken me?" (Ps 22:2).

Just as praise is not the same as thanksgiving, so lament is not identical with petition. If praise is a spontaneous response to the blessedness of life—a loud religious Wow, lament is a spontaneous response to the incursion of death in our lives. Death, as we have seen, involves not simply the moment when we breathe our last. Rather, it is the whole realm of brokenness that affects our lives on all levels and in all manifold relationships. When we experience the pain of such brokenness, we lament. Lament is a loud, religious Ouch!

Laments of one kind or another are the single largest group of psalms (over one-third or approximately fifty). Outside of the Psalms, the Books of Job and Lamentations are good examples. We find something similar in the New Testament as well. People who are afflicted cry out to Jesus (e.g. Mark 1:40-42; 7:25-30; 10:46-52). Jesus laments to the Father in the garden (Matt 26:38-39; Mark 14:34-36; Luke 22:41-44), and, in the death throes on the cross (Matt 27:46; Mark 15:34), Jesus makes his own the words of Psalm 22, cited above.

Laments are addressed directly to God (e.g., 6:2; 10:1; 12:1). They go, as it were, straight to the head office. God, however, seems very far away (4:2; 22:2). Heartfelt questions are addressed: "How long, O Lord?" (6:4; 13:1-3) which implies: I am at the end of my rope; I cannot hold on much longer; and "Why?" (10:1; 22:2), which implies: I do not understand what is going on, this is nonsense (i.e., no-meaning), a particularly distressing dimension of chaos. These are not requests for information but cries of pain.

The afflictions of the speaker(s) are described in stereotyped ways with which all sufferers can identify: sickness (6:2; 13:3; 22:14-15), loneliness and alienation (31:11; 38:11), danger and mistreatment by others (6:8; 7:1-4), shame and humiliation

(4:2; 22:6-7). Finally, the ultimate affliction is physical death (28:1; 88). All of these are manifestations of the realm of death, invading and pulling our lives apart.

Laments often speak of enemies. At times these are ene-mies from outside the community, "foreigners," "the nations" (e.g., 18:45-46; 79:1-7; 83:1-18; 144:7). At other times, it is an enemy from within who schemes and plots against the psalmist (e.g., 7:14; 27:1; 31:13). On more than one occasion, the psalmist suggests to God things that God might do to these enemies; these are the so-called "cursing" psalms (e.g., 6:11; 10:15; 28:5; 58:10-12; 109:6-19; 137:9).[11]

It is fairly obvious that as Christians we are not at all com-fortable speaking our pains, our doubts, and our anger before God. Lament leaves us uneasy; we have lost touch with this dimension of prayer, and this has been a "costly loss."[12] There would seem to be at least two main reasons for this: (1) we think that lamenting is against faith, or (2) we think that it is against charity.

(1) We feel, "My God, why have you forsaken me," and we think, "I should not feel this way; I am losing my faith." Lament corrects a false, naive, and overly rationalistic view of faith. In the Scriptures, faith is not simply an intellectual assent to some statement about God. It is trusting our entire selves to God. At times we experience God's absence; we feel alone and confused and we doubt. Doubt is not opposed to faith; despair is: "I believe, help my unbelief" (Mark 9:24); and Paul tells us he was "full of doubts but never despaired" (2 Cor 4:8). Doubt is a sign that our faith is alive and kicking. It is part of the rhythm of faith itself.[13]

11. There has been much discussion of enemies in the Psalms. A good place to begin reading on this subject would be T. R. Hobbs & P. K. Jackson, "The Enemy in the Psalms," *BTB* 21 (1991) 22–29, and the bib-liography cited there.

12. W. Brueggemann, "The Costly Loss of Lament," *JSOT* 36 (1986) 57–71. Among other works by Brueggemann on lament see "From Hurt to Joy, From Death to Life," *Int* 28 (1974) 3–19 (this whole January 1974 issue of *Int* is on lament); "The Formfulness of Grief," *Int* 31 (1977) 263–75. In recovering biblical lament, C. Westermann has made major con-tributions; see his summary in *Elements* 167–74.

13. On the centrality and importance of doubt, see R. Davidson, *The*

Lament is not a failure of faith but an act of faith. We cry out directly to God because deep down we know that our relationship with God counts; it counts to us and it counts to God. Even if we do not experience the closeness, we believe that God does care. Even if God seems not to hear, we believe that God is always within shouting distance. God does not say, "Do not fear. I will take away all the pain and struggle." Rather we hear, "Do not fear for I am with you" (e.g., to Jacob, Gen 26:24; to the anxious Moses, Exod 3:11-12; to the disciples, Matt 28:20), and together we will make it. We will survive, yes, even death itself. There is something here we need to relearn. Perhaps it is not lamenting but the failure to lament that expresses a lack of faith.

(2) We feel, against people who hurt us, "Happy the man who shall seize and smash your little ones against the rock" (137:9), and we think, "I should not feel this way; it is against charity." Lament corrects a false, naive, and overly romantic view of charity. Charity does not mean that everything is lovely, that we never get upset, that we sit around holding hands and saying how wonderful everything is. This is unreal. Negativity, injustice, brokenness are part of our lives. Charity does not deny this; it says, What next? I do feel the hurt, the pain, the anger, but this does not give me permission to go out and dump my negativity wherever and on whomever I want. Lament suggests that we dump it on God.[14]

Courage to Doubt: Exploring an Old Testament Theme (London: SCM Press, 1983).

14. On expressing anger (at God and others) in prayer, see, e.g., S. Carney, "God Damn God: A Reflection on Expressing Anger in Prayer,"*BTB* 13 (1983) 116–20; C. Christ, "Expressing Anger to God," *Anima* 5 (1978) 3–10. Commenting on the "offense" some Christians take at these psalms, L. Legrand notes: "A certain supercilious attitude towards the Old Testament in the name of 'Christian love' is in fact pseudo-Christian: it is just a continuation of the disastrous anaemic sentimentalism that does not want to look beyond the pallid range of experience of bourgeois decency and refuses to look squarely at a world ruled by violence, strife, injustice, anguish. All the talk about 'incarnational theology' is empty verbiage if it refuses to cast its roots in the dirty soil of the incarnation." *Indian Theological Studies* 14 (1979) 349.

In this light, the "cursing" psalms make sense. They have often been a particular stumbling block. We need to recognize, first, that they are clearly spoken out of great pain and distress. This is real; the feelings are really in these psalms, and at times they are really in us. But, second, the psalmist does not say, "I am going to go out and smash his little one's against the rock." We do not, as it were, take things into our own hands. We say rather, "God, this is the way I feel; You take care of it." And God has never been known to rush out and do everything we ask of him when we are angry. We let God deal with it, and in the process we get the feelings out of us. It is true that Jesus' example teaches us to pray "Father, forgive them for they know not what they do" (Luke 23:34), an attitude found also in some parts of the Old Testament (e.g., Exod 23:4-5; Prov 20:22; 24:17; 25:21-22; Job 31:29-30). This is the direction in which we hope to move. But our feelings may not always be there. Again, the feelings are real and will not go away, and if we do not recognize them and deal with them constructively, they will be heard, but destructively. Lament is a constructive way to deal with them.[15]

It has often been noted that almost all of the lament psalms (psalm 88 is an exception) end on a sudden turn to praise (e.g., 6:9-11; 10:16-18; 22:23-32; 28:6-9). Scholars have offered various explanation for this,[16] but from a prayerful viewpoint, the meaning seems clear: it is only after we lament, after we face and express the pain and negativity, that healing can begin. The power and blessing of life is experienced anew. The psalms of narrative praise (individual thanksgivings) are extensions of this turn to praise. In more theological terms, we can say that it is only by facing and going through death that we come to

15. A sample of the large literature on praying the cursing psalms would include: E. Achtemeier, *Preaching from the Old Testament* (Louisville, Ky.: Westminster/John Knox Press, 1989) 142–44; J. Blenkinsopp, "Can We Pray the Cursing Psalms," in *A Sketchbook of Biblical Theology* (London: Burns & Oates, 1968) 83–87; J. Craghan, *The Psalms*, 137–40; J. J. Greehy, "Theology Forum: The Cursing Psalms," *The Furrow* 29 (1978) 170–74; C. Stuhlmueller, *The Psalms I*. Old Testament Message 21 (Collegeville, Minn.: Liturgical Press, 1983) 312–15.

16. W. Brueggemann, "From Hurt to Joy," 8–10 surveys these opinions.

resurrection, new life. The structure of lament tells us that it is possible to praise too soon.[17] Perhaps it is not lamenting, but the failure to lament that expresses a lack of charity.

It is true that we have lost a healthy sense of lamentation in our personal prayer life. It is also true that we have lost it in our communal, liturgical prayer life. Almost the only remaining context in which lament is formally acknowledged is the funeral liturgy, but here too it is possible to give lament short shrift. Some years back, after the changes in the rite for funerals, a family I knew lost a child in a boating accident. A lot of pressure was brought to bear to "celebrate the Mass of the resurrection, to rejoice in his birth to new life." About a year later, their suppressed grief almost tore the family apart. It could not be denied and had to be dealt with. Christian faith does proclaim a message of hope, but death and grief are still real.[18]

Perhaps other situations exist in which some form of communal liturgical or paraliturgical lament would be appropriate: after a painful experience of divorce; in a religious community when dear members choose to leave; when missionaries return home after many years of service in a foreign country; in a neighborhood which has been taken over by drug dealers; in a community hard hit by HIV and AIDS; in a community devastated by natural disaster (e.g., fire, flood, earthquake, etc.); in countries where government policies or neglect break down the quality of life of its citizens; for women after the experience of rape. Others could surely be added. How helpful it would be if we had some structures to allow us to express and acknowledge grief, pain, and anger; to offer each other strength and support; and to move forward with the task and challenge of life.[19]

17. Some charismatic prayer which would praise God for everything needs to be careful in this regard.

18. S. Brown, "Bereavement in New Testament Perspective," *Worship* 48 (1974) 93–98; J. P. Meier, "Catholic Funerals in the Light of Scripture," *Worship* 48 (1974) 206–16; R. Sparkes and R. Rutherford, "The Order of Christian Funerals: A Study in Bereavement and Lament," *Worship* 60 (1986) 499–510.

19. See the discussion of G. Ramshaw, "The Place of Lament Within Praise: Theses for Discussion," *Worship* 61 (1987) 317–22, esp. thesis 3, p. 320.

The Cycle of Prayer

The prayer of the Psalms circulates around the poles of praise and lament which are rooted in real experiences of life and death. This movement of the Psalms has been described in terms of orientation (psalms of descriptive praise—creation, wisdom, royal psalms), disorientation (lament), and reorientation (narrative praise/individual thanksgiving).[20] This perspective is both helpful and insightful as long as we do not downplay or disregard the positive value of the psalms of orientation.[21] Disorientation and reorientation both represent moments of high emotional intensity; we do not live most of our lives at such moments. We can pray just as really and just as authentically at any point on the cycle.[22]

The prayer of the Psalms is rooted squarely in our lives with their ups and downs and in-betweens.[23] In stark contrast to some approaches to prayer, the Psalms are full of body and full of feeling. They are responses to God from the midst of our lives. If we are having trouble with prayer, we can begin by asking some questions: What do we mean by prayer? Does prayer include the spontaneous ouches or wows (these can be big or small) of our lives? Do we pray things that we really do not feel? Are we in touch with our experience and pray it with integrity?[24] Such questions may not solve all our prob-

20. W. Brueggemann, "Psalms and the Life of Faith: A Suggested Typology of Function," *JSOT* 17 (1980) 3–32; this distinction structures his later book, *The Message of the Psalms* (Minneapolis, Minn.: Augsburg, 1984).

21. Consistent with his negative evaluation of the blessing trajectory, Brueggemann does do this: "Psalms and the Life of Faith," 6–7; *Message*, 25–28. This was already noticed and some critique given by J. Goldingay, "The Dynamic Cycle of Praise and Prayer in the Psalms," *JSOT* 20 (1981) 85–90. Curiously Goldingay uses "Prayer" in his title where one would expect "Lament." For a balanced treatment of the orientation psalms, see J. Craghan, *The Psalms*, chaps. 2–5, pp. 24–112.

22. It is in the periods of orientation, when the emotional pitch is lower, that the older "methods of prayer" may retain their usefulness.

23. In J. Craghan's happy phrasing, *The Psalms: Prayers for the Ups, Downs and In-Betweens of Life*.

24. The biblical figure of Job presents a challenging example of integrity in prayer. See M. Guinan, *Job*, Collegeville Bible Commentary 19

lems, but they can at least point us in a direction. Prayer in the Psalms is fully and intensely human. Nothing in our human experience is beyond prayer. It is there during the everyday interactions of our lives—in our deeply felt blessings and joys, and the deeply suffered pains and hurts—that we respond to our God, the source and root of our life. We can do nothing more; we should do nothing less.

(Collegeville, Minn.: The Liturgical Press, 1986) 82–83; in the one volume edition, *The Collegeville Bible Commentary* (Collegeville, Minn.: The Liturgical Press, 1989) 699.

Chapter 6

Keep Holy the Sabbath

At the beginning of the Bible, in the first chapters of Genesis, we find an account of God's creating (Gen 1:1-2:4). In the beginning, the world is in disordered chaos—dark, watery, formless, and void. This is the way the ancients conceived the pole opposite the existing world. (Later philosophers and theologians would conceive of this same opposite pole as *nothingness*.) Then the creator God begins to subdue the chaos and to call out an ordered universe. This creative activity continues through the six-day week, culminating on the seventh day: "Thus the heavens and the earth and all their array were completed. Since on the seventh day God was finished with the work he had been doing, he rested on the seventh day" (Gen 2:1-2). At the beginning was chaos; at the climax was sabbath rest.

Just as the days of the week move forward to a goal, so also does human history.[1] Sabbath rest is a foreshadowing, an imaging of that goal. In chapter four, we looked at life, peace, and justice as expressing God's goal and purpose for humans and all of creation. We can now explore the image of sabbath, looking first at sabbath in the Bible, and then at some aspects of a sabbath spirituality.

Sabbath in the Bible

Israel had a calendar of feasts to help it recognize and celebrate the sacredness of time (Lev 23). The regular, weekly ob-

1. C. Westermann, *Elements of Old Testament Theology* (Atlanta, Ga.: John Knox Press, 1982) 94.

servance of the Sabbath was of special importance, an importance which continues in Judaism down to the present.[2]

Why Rest?

We can begin by asking, Why did Israel celebrate the Sabbath? We find not one answer but two. The command to keep holy the Sabbath is by far the longest of the Ten Commandments (Exod 20:8-11; Deut 5:12-25), and the two accounts are very similar until the reason for keeping the Sabbath is given. In Deuteronomy (5:15) we read, "For remember that you too were once slaves in Egypt, and the LORD, your God, brought you from there with his strong hand and outstretched arm. That is why the Lord, your God, has commanaded you to observe the sabbath day." Israel is to keep the Sabbath in order to remember that Yahweh saved them from Egypt. They were enslaved and oppressed, and Yahweh delivered them. Now every seventh day serves to remind Israel that Yahweh is a God who liberates from oppression and calls to freedom. All of Israel's life and time is a gift of the saving God.

When we turn to Exodus (20:11), we find a completely different reason. There we find, "In six days the LORD made the heavens and the earth, the sea and all that is in them; but on the seventh day he rested. That is why the Lord has blessed the sabbath day and made it holy." Israel rests in order to share God's sabbath rest of creation, when God "blessed the seventh day and made it holy" (Gen 2:3). Previously, human beings—man and woman—had been created and blessed and given their twofold command (Gen 1:26-28). But God does not say, "OK, now you're created to share my work, so get to it!" The first full human day (as well as that of all creation)

---

2. For what follows, see especially M. Guinan, *The Pentateuch.* Message of Biblical Spirituality 1 (Collegeville, Minn.: The Liturgical Press, 1990) 77–79; H. W. Wolff, *Anthropology of the Old Testament* (Philadelphia, Pa.: Fortress Press, 1974) 134–42; J. Siker-Gieseler, "The Theology of the Sabbath in the Old Testament: A Canonical Approach," *Studia Biblica et Theologica* 11 (1981) 5–20; A. Heschel, *The Sabbath* (New York: Farrar, Straus & Giroux, 1975).

was the seventh day of rest. God's week culminated with the Sabbath; the human week begins with it.[3]

The two motives speak from the two covenant theologies, one a theology of blessing, the other, one of saving. But they belong together and interpret each other. "God's creative activity is liberating, and God's activity as liberator is creative."[4] Keeping the Sabbath is an act of memory.

Who Rests?

The obvious answer to the question, Who rests? is: *I* do. But, as we have seen so often, the individual exists only in relationships, so that *my* rest will have an affect on these relationships as well. Thus, "you and your son and your daughter, your male and female slaves, your animals, the alien who lives with you" (Exod 20:10; 23:12; Deut 5:14) all share the Sabbath rest. All those persons whose lives are intertwined with mine—family, household, even aliens—are involved. The animals are also affected and share in this rest. But it does not stop here. The very earth itself shares the Sabbath, in the sabbatical (seventh) year (Exod 23:10-11; Lev 25:2-7).

Our Sabbath rest expresses an awareness of the interconnectedness of our lives with other people, with the animals, and with the natural world itself. We live from God's creating and liberating activity and are called, as images and servants, to extend and share this activity in and through all of our relationships. Keeping the Sabbath is an act of solidarity.

When to Rest?

We are to celebrate the Sabbath every week, every seventh day; thus the sharing in the blessing of God's rest becomes part of the regular rhythm of our time and our lives. In addition to every week, every seventh year is a sabbatical year which involves the land in a special way (Exod 23:10-11; Lev 25:2-7), and every forty-ninth year (seven times seven) is the grand year of Jubilee when the land lies at rest, property is returned

3. C. Westermann, *Elements*, 94; H. W. Wolff, *Anthropology*, 138.

4. J. Siker-Gieseler, "Theology of the Sabbath," 16.

to its original owner, and slaves are set free (Lev 25:8-55).[5] The Sabbath is not meant to be an isolated occurrence, but is to be woven into the rhythms and patterns of the weeks and the years.

What about times that are especially crucial or difficult? Are we to rest then? Israel is wandering in the wilderness; in their hunger they cry out to God who hears their cry and gives them manna. "On the sixth day they gathered twice as much food . . . (Moses) told them, 'That is what the LORD prescribed. Tomorrow is a day of complete rest, the sabbath, sacred to the LORD . . .'" (Exod 16:22-23). Even in the wilderness, they are to keep the Sabbath. Later, they settle in the land; then, the most important times are those of planting and harvesting. Food for the whole year depends on these. Yet, "For six days you may work, but on the seventh day you shall rest; on that day you must rest even during the seasons of plowing and harvesting" (Exod 34:21). Here too Israel is to keep the Sabbath.

Celebrating the Sabbath is inserted into the patterns and regularities of our lives, even in times of need (the saving bread, manna; the blessing bread, produce of the soil). We often think everything depends on us; we can forget all too easily who is really the Source of all. Our lives, our work, our time are— and continue to be—in the hands of the creating, saving God. Keeping the Sabbath is an act of faith.

The New Testament

While in the Old Testament the Sabbath already had an aspect of foreshadowing the fullness God intends for Israel and all of creation, i.e., an eschatological element (e.g. Isa 56:2-7), this element appears even more strongly in the New Testament. Rest is a sharing in the kingdom which Jesus both preaches and realizes in his person.

---

5. For a discussion of the liberating aspects of the jubilee year, see R. Gnuse, *You Shall Not Steal: Community and Property in the Biblical Tradition* (Maryknoll, N.Y.: Orbis Books, 1985) 32–47; S. H. Ringe, *Jesus, Liberation, and the Biblical Jubilee: Images for Ethics and Christology* (Philadelphia, Pa.: Fortress Press, 1985).

A number of Jesus' controversies with the Jewish leaders of his day, appearing in all four Gospels, was over the meaning of the Sabbath. The relatively few actual prescriptions of the Old Testament for Sabbath observance had been so expanded that what was supposed to be a joyous celebration of freedom had become a heavy burden. Whether it was working on the Sabbath (e.g. Mark 2:23-28; Matt 12:1-8; Luke 6:1-5), or healing (Mark 3:1-6; Matt 12:1-14; Luke 6:6-11; John 5:1-18; 7:22-24; 9:13-17), Jesus is Lord of the Sabbath which is subordinated to his work and his kingdom. "The sabbath's purpose, as Jesus sees it, is fulfilled not by forbidding works of compassion, but by encouraging them."[6] In Genesis, God had blessed the Sabbath and made it holy, i.e., had filled it with life-giving power; Jesus' work was to restore this. In a real sense, he revitalized the Sabbath.

Jesus is the source of rest. He calls to those who are weary and overburdened, "Come to me . . . and I will give you rest. Take my yoke upon you and learn from me, for I am meek and humble of heart; and you will find rest for yourselves" (Matt 11:28-30). And immediately after this (12:1-14) we have two incidents of Jesus involved in controversy about the Sabbath.

Another feature that occurs in all four Gospels is that Jesus would often retire by himself to pray. "Rising very early before dawn, he left and went off to a deserted place, where he prayed" (Mark 1:35); ". . . he went up on the mountain by himself to pray" (Matt 14:23); "The report about him spread all the more, and great crowds assembled to listen to him and to be cured of their ailments, but he would withdraw to deserted places to pray" (Luke 5:15-16; also 6:12; 9:28-29); "Since Jesus knew that they were going to come and carry him off to make him king, he withdrew again to the mountain alone" (John 6:15). In the midst of his ministry of preaching and healing, Jesus took the time to withdraw and find rest alone with God.

The Epistle to the Hebrews (3:7-4:11) gives a reflection on the Sabbath commandment and Psalm 95 in the light of Christ.

6. R. J. Karris, "The Gospel of Luke," *NJBC* 43:139.

"A sabbath rest still remains for the people of God" (Heb 4:9). Those who are faithful to God will enter into God's sabbath rest. They will share the "rest" of heaven.[7] A similar theme is found in the Book of Revelation. Those who fall into idolatry and worship the beast shall have "no rest day or night," but those who die in the Lord will be blessed and "find rest from their labors" (Rev 14:11,13).

The theme of sabbath rest runs as a rich theme through both the Old and New Testaments. In the New, Jesus' revitalizing of the Sabbath sheds important light on the meaning of his teaching and person. Rest is an image of the fullness of life with God.

A Sabbath Spirituality

In light of the meaning of the Sabbath in the Bible, a number of significant perceptions may be highlighted:[8]

(1) We live in a work-driven society. *Doing* is all important, and we are worth what we do (and what we are paid for doing it). We grow weary, wear down, come unglued, and when we get time for rest, we do not quite know what to do with it. When we try to relax and play cards or play sports, the overriding competitive drive of the culture pervades them and they become occasions for stress and tension. More than one observer has noted the grim determination with which Americans have fun.[9]

7. M. Bourke, "The Epistle to the Hebrews," *NJBC* 60:23-24; H. Attridge, "Epistle to the Hebrews," *Harper's Bible Commentary*, J. L. Mays, ed. (San Francisco, Calif.: Harper & Row, 1988) 1263.

8. Among a number of works which have appeared with similar concerns, see M. J. Dawn, *Keeping the Sabbath Wholly: Ceasing, Resting, Embracing, Feasting* (Grand Rapids, Mich.: Wm. B. Eerdmans, 1989); T. J. Edwards, "The Christian Sabbath: Its Promise Today As A Basic Spiritual Discipline," *Worship* 56 (1982) 2-15; *Sabbath's Time: Understanding and Practice for Contemporary Christians* (San Francisco, Calif.: Harper & Row, 1984).

9. This phrasing is from anthropologist J. Henry, *Culture Against Man* (New York: Vintage Press, 1965) 43. See also K. Woodward, "What is Leisure Anyhow? If Only Americans Could Just Learn To Relax," *Newsweek* (August 26, 1991) 56.

Those whose work is in public ministry—clergy, religious, lay persons—face special challenges. Since their work "for the kingdom" brings them into constant contact with people in suffering and need as well as into conflict with social structures which cause or contribute to that suffering, taking time "to rest" can seem like shirking one's call. However, the need for rest is here even more acute. "Burn out" is an occupational hazard, and whether one burns out pursuing fame and fortune or burns out in working for the kingdom, one is still burnt out.[10]

(2) In our work we are pulled in many directions; we become scattered and come apart. We need to gather ourselves back together; we need *re-collection*. We need to re-root ourselves in our vision so that it can exercise its unifying, integrating force on our lives. What is our underlying motivation? It is all too easy to lose sight of what we are doing, where we are going, and why.

The image of a mountain climber is sometimes proposed. Climbers have to look very closely at what is right in front of them; where they put their feet; where they grab with their hands. Every now and then, they pause and rest and may well ask themselves, What am I doing here anyway? But then they look up; the clouds part (and the violins play), and they see the peak, and this pulls them forward again. We live by, out of, and into our vision.

The need for prayer, recollection, and solitude in our lives as Christians is clear. They should be part of the regular rhythms of our time: daily, weekly, monthly, yearly. Whether it is a matter of minutes, an hour or so, a day here or there, an annual retreat—like Jesus, even in the midst of the needs

10. J. J. Gill, "Burn Out: A Growing Threat in Ministry," *Human Development* 1/2 (Summer 1980) 21–27; A. M. Pines, *Burnout: From Tedium to Personal Growth* (New York: Free Press, 1981); the national office of Catholic Bishops in the United States, through its Committee on Priestly Life and Ministry, addressed this question in a very helpful document, *The Priest and Stress* (Washington, D.C.: USCC Publishing, 1982). While this is concerned explicitly with priests, what is said can be applied much more broadly.

of the crowds—we need to get away. Rest and recollection are acts of faith.

(3) We have just used the image of coming apart and *re-collecting*. Another image, with biblical roots, shows us a different side of rest. We become *dis-ordered*; we return, as it were, to chaos. We need *re-ordering* or creating again. We need *re-creation*. Regular recreation of some kind, alone or with others, would seem essential for good physical, mental, and spiritual health. The problem, noted above, is that so often recreation can become just another source of stress.

God creates and says, "Let there be. . . ." We are so busy in our lives with doing, making, dominating, competing . . . do we know what it means to let things be? Can we just sit back and relax and let be? Our ability to do this can affect greatly the quality of our lives. A special role can be played by the arts in helping us to do this. Beauty—in nature, in music, painting, sculpture, film, literature, theater, dance, or whatever—both enriches our experience and puts us in touch with transcendence, a transcendence which finds its root in God, our "crown of beauty" (Isa 28:5).

What do you do with a sunset? You enjoy it. With a song? You sing it. With a dance? You dance it. How do you use beauty? You do not; rather you are filled with it, respond to it, let it be.[11] This includes the vision of beauty we may see and be invited to produce ourselves, in whatever medium. The role of the artist in spirituality is one we have underestimated.

As God created the universe, the refrain repeated over and over again is, ". . . and God saw that it was good." Too often we understand this "good" in some vague moralistic way. The Hebrew word used there (*tob*) could just as well be translated *beautiful*; ". . . and God saw how beautiful it was!"[12] As im-

11. On the distinction between using and enjoying and its implications in theology and spirituality, see F. Baur, *Life in Abundance* (Ramsey, N.J.: Paulist Press, 1983) 106–9.

12. C. Westermann, *Elements*, 93. Since beauty belongs primarily to the blessing theological tradition, it too has suffered neglect. It is a topic ripe for a thorough study. As a beginning, see M. Guinan, "In the Beginning—Beauty," *Creation* 1/6 (Jan 1986) 22–23; W. A. Dryness, "Aesthetics in the Old Testament: Beauty in Context," *JETS*

ages of God who share with God the bringing of order and
harmony out of chaos and disorder, we need to envision and
invite, to "let be" a more beautiful world. This beauty is
manifested in the works of nature all around us and in the
artifacts we are invited to produce. It will be experienced and
manifested also and above all in the beauty of our own lives
and of our social orders as we strive to embody a vision of
beauty (another term which—like life, peace, and justice—
has to do with harmonious relationships). Jesus invites us to
let our "beautiful works" shine out like the light on the first
day of creation (Matt 5:16).[13]

(4) Often, to describe resting, the expression is used, "killing
time." This betrays a complete misunderstanding of the meaning of rest. Rest is "enlivening time." Rest is not for work; it
is for life. Work so dominates our concerns that everything
tends to be seen in relation to it; thus, we work and work and
then grow tired, so we have to stop and rest in order to go
back to work. This attitude is especially insidious regarding
our work for the kingdom of God. When push comes to shove,
many of us are crypto-Pelagian. It is God's work, and if we
stop to rest, God is still there. If we do not stop to celebrate
this, we may not be able to do anybody's work for very long;
we burn out.

A group of priests were together in the mountains by a lake.
They were classmates and, over the years, had tried to take
at least some time together on their vacations. The weather
was perfect; one was a good cook. They fished, swam, hiked,
prayed together. The time came to leave, and they were load-
ing the car. One looked around at the beautiful scene, sighed
and said, "Well, back to reality!" There was a pause; they

28 (1985) 421–32; C. Westermann, "Das Schöne im Alten Testament,"
*Beiträge zur alttestamentlichen Theologie: Festschrift für W. Zimmerli
zum 70 Geburtstag,* H. Donner, et al., eds. (Göttingen: Vandenhoeck
& Ruprecht, 1977) 479–97. On the false dichotomy between a con-
cern for beauty and social justice, see the wise words of R. Hovda,
"The Amen Corner: Scripture Has It, Not on Bread Alone Shall Human
Creatures Live," *Worship* 57 (1983) 255–63.
    13. M. Guinan, "In the Beginning-Beauty," 23.

looked at each other and simultaneously realized, "That is backwards. *This* is reality. What we are going back to is less than reality."[14]

We need to rest—and celebrate that rest—so we do not become confused about what is reality and what is less. The purpose of our work is to move the "less" more and more into reality. Our moments of rest are not lows when we regain our strength to go back up into work; they are highs when we recontact and renew our vision of what reality is all about (see Illustration 6.1). Then we go down into the everyday with clearer vision. Much sin, injustice, and brokenness exists in the world; many people can agree on this. But what is the solution? How do we move into greater wholeness? Our periods of rest—individual and communal—are essential to keeping our vision of God's kingdom of justice, peace, and life.[15]

In the Philippines (the custom is practiced in other cultures as well), each town or barrio has its patron saint and once a year celebrates its barrio-fiesta. The people, living mostly from farming and fishing, save up all year for the big event. When the several days of celebrating are over, life resumes again. On occasion, outsiders (often Americans) will say something like, "What a waste of money and resources; if you used the same money in different ways, you could raise the standard of living here in different ways!" As one elderly Filipino told me, "They just don't understand! You can live without more things; you cannot live without fiesta." Rest is for life.[16]

(5) Finally, in this light, we might say a word on behalf of a neglected virtue: Christian *selfishness*. We say so easily, "Love your neighbor as yourself," and "Charity begins at home," but is it that easy? We spend considerably more time on improving our *well-doing*; we are less concerned about our well-being. Being well has a number of dimensions: physical,

14. A. Kavanaugh, *On Liturgical Theology* (New York: Pueblo Publishing, 1984) 151–76, gives a profound discussion of this point: in the liturgy we experience "normality" which puts in perspective the "abnormality" of our everyday world.

15. The role of the liturgy is, of course, essential. We will comment more on this in the next chapter.

16. This is the main point of R. Hovda, "Amen Corner," 255–63.

psychological, intellectual, aesthetic, spiritual; and they are all connected and interacting. It is, of course, quite possible to care for ourselves out of purely selfish motives—our culture and its advertisements are full of incentives to do just this—but it need not be so. Our call to imagehood includes proper stewardship of God's first gift to each of us, ourselves.[17]

In the first narrative of the Bible, God creates a universe, harmonious and habitable, and fills it with living beings. Humans come at the climax of that creation and are charged to share God's work. But the human work in the world begins by sharing in God's sabbath rest. As the narrative progresses we see human failure, individually, socially, cosmically. The road to fulness will be long and difficult, but human time is punctuated by stopping to celebrate Sabbath, to remember the gifts of the creating, saving God and the goal that God has for all. The work and person of Jesus stands at the center, calling to come to him for rest (Matt 11:28). Human work in the world ends by sharing fully in God's sabbath rest (Heb 3:7–4:11; Rev 14:13). We need to recover a healthy spirituality of rest.

17. C. R. Berry & M. L. Taylor, *Loving Yourself as Your Neighbor: A Recovery Guide for Christians Escaping Burnout and Codependency* (San Francisco, Calif.: Harper & Row, 1990). This same point is recognized and addressed by the Bishops' Committee in *Priests and Stress, 3.*

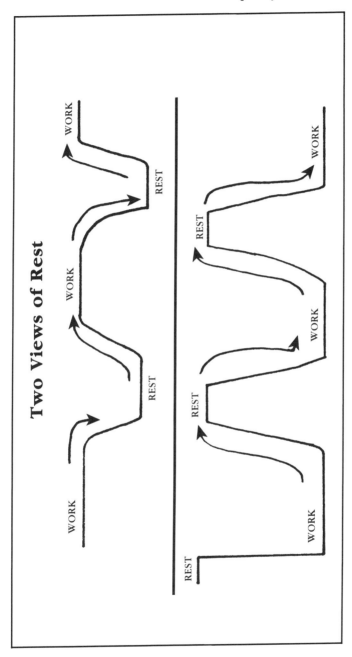

Two Views of Rest

WORK REST WORK REST WORK

REST WORK REST WORK REST WORK

Illustration 6.1

Chapter 7

Eucharist: An Act of Memory

As we come to the end of our study of and reflection upon some central issues of biblical spirituality, a summary of some kind is in order. We have close at hand a means to help us do this: the Eucharist. When we gather together to worship as God's people, almost all of the things we have so far discussed come into focus. By way, then, of summary and review, we will offer some observations and comments on the Eucharist, not looking at every detail, but following its overall movement and action.

The Setting and Gathering

In the midst of our everyday and ordinary time, we set aside a special time for rest. Above all, this takes place on the Day of the Resurrection. Like all of the religious institutions of ancient Israel, the Sabbath has been transformed in and through Christ. The Christian Sabbath is the eighth day, the day of the new creation. On this day of rest, we gather to reroot ourselves in reality, in normalcy.

We gather in a special place set apart for our worship. This should be a place of beauty. Architecture, painting, sculpture, stained glass, banners: all these contribute to the quality of our experience of space. Later on, music (vocal, instrumental) and, on occasion, dance make their contributions. The role of the arts in our worship, as should be in our lives, is significant.[1]

At this time and into this space, we gather. We come together, not on our own initiative and for our own ends, but

1. On beauty and the liturgy, see A. Dulles, *The Catholicity of the Church* (Oxford: Clarendon Press, 1985) 55.

because we are responding to a call. God, who creates us and
redeems us, has first called us. In both Hebrew and Greek, the
words for assembly/community (*qahal, ekklesia*) come from
roots meaning "to call." As the Christian community, we are
"called out" by God; we gather in humble and loving response
to that call.

Who comes to worship? *I* do, and not the isolated, in-
dividualistic I, but the related I. I gather with other people;
some of them I know, some I do not; with some of them I get
along and agree; with some of them I may not. But we come
together as one, united in our faith and response to God.
Animals are not usually part of our worship (in the tropical
climate of the Philippines, where the church walls are largely
open, it is not uncommon to have birds, dogs, and cats present, with chickens, pigs, and water buffalo visible in the sur-
rounding fields—are we missing something?), but natural
creation is present: flowers often decorate our churches; we
find blessed water as we enter; and later we will share bread
and wine. It is the whole *I* who gathers for worship.

The Table of the Word

We then hear our story proclaimed from the Scriptures.
It is the "big story" of God and the world and history in the
context of which the "little story" of my life makes sense. We
hear of God's creative activity and God's liberating activity;
sometimes the readings focus more on one, at other times, on
the other. We hear the word of prophetic challenge and critique of our lives and our societies; we hear their consolation
in times of distress. We always hear of the life, person, work,
and teaching of Jesus, the full image and perfect servant, in
whose image we try to live. In and through these readings,
we recapture our identity: who we are, where we are from,
where we are going, and how we are to get there. We also
realize who we are *not*, or at least, *not yet*. The vision of life,
peace, and justice sits in judgment on us and our societies of
whatever time and place. In the light of God's call, we realize
how little we have done and how far we have to go. The vision draws us ever forward. We are involved as individuals,
as societies, and as a cosmos.

The Word is proclaimed. We are supposd to listen. In the Bible, the primary organ of hearing is not the ear, though this is where the sound enters, but the heart. If the Word goes in one ear and out the other we have not heard. The Word is to penetrate into our hearts, the very center of ourselves. If we turn away our hearts, we do not listen (Deut 30:17). If we are hardhearted, the Word cannot enter and take effect. "O, that today you would hear his voice, 'Harden not your hearts . . .' " (Ps 95:8). It is not accidental that in Hebrew, Greek, Latin, and English (based on the Latin), the words for *obedience* come from roots for *listening*. To hear, listen with the whole heart means that we allow the Word of God to enter deeply into our inner selves, the very core of our persons. As a result we are changed.[2]

While we ponder the readings, a psalm is sung. It may be a prayer of praise or one of lament, reflecting some aspect of the readings for the liturgy. The homily seeks both to deepen our understanding of the Scriptures and to apply them to our concrete times and places. In the prayers of intercession we can give expression to both our praises and laments. These are shared with and entered into by all in the community.

The Table of the Lord's Supper

We move to celebrate together the Lord's Supper. Bread and wine are brought forward and prepared, gifts that represent us and our lives. The prayer over them proclaims, "Blessed are you, Lord, God of all creation. Through your goodness we have this bread/wine to offer, which earth has given/fruit of the vine and human hands have made/and work of human hands. It will become for us the bread of life/our spiritual drink." This is clearly blessing bread and drink: the produce of the earth and the work of human hands. Both are needed if we are to have bread; unlike manna, it does not fall from heaven.

"Lift up your hearts . . . It is right to give the Lord thanks and praise." The Eucharistic Prayer is a prayer of praise. We

2. See M. Guinan, *The Pentateuch*. Message of Biblical Spirituality 1. (Collegeville, Minn.: The Liturgical Press, 1990) 103–5.

remember and recount what God has done for us. We focus on the Giver and the gift; we are the recipients. We remember Jesus, and how, on the night before he died, he took the bread and the wine. "This is the blood of the new and eternal covenant shed for you and for all." Jesus' words recall the blood of the covenant at Sinai (Exod 24:6-8). Yahweh had saved Israel from Egypt: you are my people, I am your God. In Jesus' blood of the new covenant, we are all saved from sin and death and called to become a new people in the Spirit breathed out on us.

As we prepare to receive the body and blood of Christ, we pray together the prayer that Jesus taught us, the *Our Father*. We often look at this prayer as a list of petitions that we ask of God. Perhaps it can more accurately be viewed as a vision and a challenge to us. "Thy kingdom come." If God's kingdom really comes on our earth, it means that something else has to go; and our experience tells us that the kingdom of death with its sin and selfishness will not go quietly or easily. Maybe the realism of the lament psalms with their talk of enemies has something for us to learn. "Thy will be done on earth as in heaven. . . ." Who is it that should do God's will on earth if not ourselves who claim to be God's children? What would the earth look like if this were true? "Give us this day our daily bread." How does God give bread if not in and through our actions of responding to the hungers of the world? "Forgive us as we forgive." This is the way we can move to reconciliation and peace. How often and how casually we pray this prayer; it has earth-transforming implications![3]

The liturgy recognizes what we so often do not. From the *Our Father* we move to the Sign of Peace. Peace was the gift of the risen Christ on that first Easter evening (John 20:19-20), and before we come forward to receive the risen Christ, we share a sign of that peace (Matt 5:23-24). We are meant to be instruments of Christ's peace to others; we are meant to be open to receive it from others. If there is to be real peace, it

3. I owe this view of the *Our Father* to Francis Baur who develops it in *Life In Abundance: A Contemporary Spirituality* (Ramsey, N.J.: Paulist, 1983) 210–17.

will come from the Spirit working in and through us. Our ritual gesture expresses this.

As we near the time of communion, a sense of our sinfulness, weakness, and need emerges. We have prayed in the *Our Father,* "Forgive us our trespasses as we forgive others . . ." Now we say, "Lamb of God who takes away the sins of the world, have mercy on us." And just before coming forward, we will say, "Lord, I am not worthy to receive you." We are weak and sinful, and we need saving. And this is precisely why we have the Eucharist. It is not given to us as a reward for being good or as a sign of our virtue; it is a source of nourishment and strength as we try to live more completely the life in the Spirit we are called to. And like the weak and sinful Israel processing through the wilderness, we come forward in procession, a people on the march, to receive our saving bread, the true manna come down from heaven. Jesus is in our midst as both blessing bread (the preparation prayer) and saving bread (the communion). What kind of bread do we need?

Blessing and Sending

Just before we are sent out, we receive the final blessing. This is not just a prayer for God to do something; it is a last reminder of what our God is like, what God is up to and what we should be up to in our world. The first blessing listed in the missal for ordinary time is the high priestly blessing from Numbers 6:24-26. A brief reflection on it may be helpful.[4]

> May the Lord bless you
> and keep you
> May the Lord shine his face upon you
> and be gracious to you
> May the Lord look upon you with kindness
> and give you his peace.

4. On this blessing, see D. N. Freedman, "The Aaronic Benediction (Numbers 6:24-26)," in *No Famine in the Land,* J. Robinson, ed. (Missoula, Mont.: Scholars Press, 1975) 35–48; P. D. Miller, "The Blessing of God: An Interpretation of Numbers 6:22-27," *Int* 29 (1975) 240–51.

May the Lord bless you: blessing, the power of life in all its manifestations. May God fill us with life so that this will flow in and through all of our relationships.

And keep you: literally, "guard over you." Anti-life forces are about, both within us and without in the world around us. Life needs watching over, guarding, protecting, keeping. This sounds a note of warning and struggle; but "the LORD will guard (keep) you from all evil; he will guard your life" (Ps 121:7).

May the Lord shine his face upon you: the somber note continues. Darkness belongs to the kingdom of death. God's first move in subduing the chaos at the beginning is to say, "Let there be light." The light of God brings salvation. The psalmist prays, "Let your face shine upon us so that we shall be saved" (Ps 80:4, 8, 20); "Let your face shine upon your servant, save me in your kindness" (Ps 31:17).

And be gracious to you: more frequently in the Psalms this same expression is translated, "have pity on us" and is common in contexts of lament (e.g., 6:3). In our weakness and need we call on the Lord who is compassionate and filled with pity towards us.

May the Lord look upon you with kindness: in the Hebrew this is literally, "May the LORD lift up his face to you." One of the sources of pain and confusion in laments is that God's face is hidden. We feel alone and forsaken: "When you hid your face, I was terrified" (Ps 30:8; cf. 10:11; 22:25). We pray to enjoy again the presence of God.

And give you peace: shalom, the wholeness and integrity of relationships with self, others, the world, and God.

Like the Bible itself which begins with the blessing of creation and ends with the peace of the new Jerusalem, this short prayer begins with blessing and ends with peace. This is God's first and last word. But in between danger lurks. There is sin and suffering and failure. The four prayers in between are all common in laments; they are prayers for saving. We are blessed, raised up and gifted; we are also weak and sinful and in need of saving.

Blessed and saved, we are sent out from the Eucharist into the world, to continue there what we have just been doing:

to be aware that we live intimately in relationship with everyone and with all of creation and with God; to reflect on the Scriptures that tell our story and remind us of who we truly are; to accept our role before God, as images and as servants; to recognize God's gifts of blessing and of saving and to speak honestly to God out of our lives; to receive from Christ strength, nourishment, consolation, and challenge; to go forth to be instruments of life, peace, justice, beauty in our lives, our societies, our world.

Being human before God is not such a bad thing. Though indeed we need saving, we are not worthless worms cluttering the earth. Though indeed we have been blessed, neither are we gods. And that is all right. We are called to be images and servants in the likeness of Jesus. It is a high and awesome calling; we should never settle for less.